AN ASCENT TO JOY

An Ascent to Joy

Transforming Deadness of Spirit

Carol Ochs

University of Notre Dame Press
Notre Dame, Indiana 46556

Quotations from the Hebrew Scriptures are from
the translation of the Jewish Publication Society.

Library of Congress Cataloging-in-Publication Data

Ochs, Carol.
  An ascent to joy.

  Bibliography: p.
  1. Spirituality. 2. Consolation. I. Title.
BL624.029 1986   291.4   85-41019
ISBN 0-268-00615-6

Manufactured in the United States of America

To Michael Ochs
with joy

Contents

Preface

There are different questions for different times in our lives. When I was about to enter graduate study, the realization that as a Jewish woman I could not enter into rabbinical training raised serious questions for me. Many years later I explored these questions in my first book, *Behind the Sex of God*. I had wanted to learn what being a woman meant in a system that differentiates so strongly between men's and women's roles. And then I came to a realization: if I could understand that it was a system that precluded my training, then I could recover or envision an alternative system. The book that resulted draws out the alternative visions of patriarchal and matriarchal world views.

Awareness of alternative world views raised new questions. Were there world views that enabled us to better come into relationship with reality? It was necessary to critique patriarchy and to suggest new possibilities, but it was not sufficient. If patriarchy was mistaken, it was so because it did not avail itself of the insights that women can contribute to our common search for a truly human, truly spiritual way of life. My second book, *Women and Spirituality*, attempts to show how women's views complement and complete traditional Western spirituality.

Preface

The concern for how we should live presupposes that
we shall live. Yet there are times when this very assump-
tion comes into question. Perhaps we are faced once too
often with the news of an impending planetary disaster;
perhaps the source of the concern is more personal. The
question, when it arises, is an urgent one. I began to explore it, but eventually came to realize that I was not
writing about the threat to the planet or even about
literal death. I had, through my earlier work, come to
appreciate the importance and validity of our own experiences, and had chosen to write only out of my experience. I do not have experience of the death of life
as we know it; I do have experience of deadness in life,
of the loss of a capacity for joy.

Much that I learned about spirituality I learned from
my dog Boris. It must seem strange to learn about something so difficult and complex from an animal, but perhaps it was his very simplicity that made me understand
more from him than I could from the complex, multi-
dimensional actions of people. Boris could not stand anger. When people raised their voices he simply walked
out of the room. He also could not believe that people
would stay angry. After he had knocked over a lamp or
soiled the rug, he simply could not believe that we were
still annoyed five minutes later. He found each day ex-
citing and with the dawn would dash up to our room
to waken us so we could share it with him. But the last
lesson Boris taught me was harder and more painful than
the others. Boris taught me what it is to grow old when
your whole life is your body and you cannot think or
be diverted from the progressive deterioration. As he
grew older, being petted was no longer fun, it hurt. He
grew deaf, could no longer use his back legs, and became disoriented.

Boris was real, and I mourned his death. But Boris

was also a powerful symbol of how we will inevitably move toward deterioration and deadness if we do not consciously work for renewal. Boris could not employ images to refresh and renew him, but we, being human, have this possibility.

This book deals with the questions that arise after we have experienced loss, sadness, disillusionment, even despair. It attempts to understand deadness and to find a way to use this experience to correct our relationship with reality and ultimately to taste the sweetness of life. While the book does not deal directly with the threat to the planet, I console myself with the mystic equation of the microcosm with the macrocosm. Perhaps when we can find renewal for our lives, we can renew the world as well.

In the process of working through mourning, sadness, and deadness, I have found continuing direction and support in the works of theologians and philosophers. The theologians whose work most informs my own are Martin Buber, John Dunne, and Abraham Joshua Heschel. The philosophers whose works remain guideposts for me are Plato and Spinoza. But by far, the texts that have consistently nourished and sustained me throughout my life are the Hebrew Scriptures.

I have learned about love, covenant, and friendship from the Bible and from the writings of Plato, Spinoza, and Buber. But I have learned even more deeply from those whose love and friendship have transformed my life. Their commitment has given me the experience of a covenant through which *the* covenant shines.

Acknowledgments

I am grateful to my students at Simmons College for continuing to enjoy exploring these questions with me; to Pamela Lloyd, for her generous gift of time and care in reading this book in manuscript; and to the members of Companions, who have taught me the deepest meaning of friendship.

AN ASCENT TO JOY

Introduction

There comes a time for most of us when the world ceases to speak to us, when we no longer have faith that it can be the setting for our fulfillment, and when we experience deadness. The cause of this deadness is often fear or pain. We protect ourselves by "psychic numbing" so as not to experience the pain and so we lose the joy as well.

My objective in this book is to discover the causes of deadness and help us recover the wonder and joy that is our natural inheritance. The world before our deadness is not essentially different from the world after our deadness. So the problem resides not in *the* world but in *our* world. Our world is related to the world at large in much the same way as our photograph of the Grand Canyon relates to the Grand Canyon. If there were no Grand Canyon, there would be no photograph. But to understand the photograph we also would have to know the type of camera used, the lens opening, the exposure time, film speed, and other technical aspects. We also must know the angle selected for the picture and what was being focused on. We brought to the Grand Canyon our experiences, our talents, our sensitivities, and our expectations. All of these make our photograph different from someone else's and different from the Grand Canyon itself.

Our world is the world as we perceive it. Our perceptions are shaped by our experiences, by our talents (especially in the domain of imagination), by our sensitivities, and by our expectations. Other people's worlds influence us just as a striking photograph might lead us to try our own hand at a new technique. We can grow in photographic artistry, and we can similarly grow in the supreme artistry of perceiving the world.

The experience of deadness is a recurring problem in the human condition. The Desert Fathers of the fourth century, who were acute observers of their own spiritual states, describe this condition and offer a remedy which is the starting point for this investigation. Their remedy is explicitly theological and, given the modern condition, we cannot accept it without tailoring it to our contemporary sensibilities. Nevertheless they offer significant clues.

The theological approach of the Desert Fathers is developed by Saint Anselm some four hundred years later. The ontological argument, for too long thought to be a proof for the existence of God, actually shows itself to be Anselm's treatment for the deadness of his fellow monks.

The experience of deadness has serious implications for religion, as recognized by the Christian Desert Fathers and by Anselm. It is recognized in the Jewish tradition as well and many of the insights offered by the Hasidim deal with the importance of joy. But the struggle against deadness can be self-defeating if we don't learn from the experience. If we explore the occasions that precipitate deadness, we find some guideposts left to us by the spiritual traditions.

We recognize the problem experientially. We must now seek an approach toward dealing with it — a way to turn darkness to light. Our most fundamental viewpoint is our own experience. We bring it to everything we do and use it to test all that we learn. If we are taught that persimmons are sweet, we may not doubt it, but we don't fully believe it until we have tasted them ourselves. Our experience tells us that we suffer deadness, and only our experience can tell us when we have found an appropriate remedy.

Just as we bring more to photography than our experiences, so we bring to life our own way of thinking about life, our angle of vision, and our choice of focus. These expectations, angles of vision, and choice of focus are what I mean by symbols. We do not think in things, we think in symbols for things. These symbols (whether they are words, images, or tactile sensations) are powerful tools and filters for our perception. We can change filters in photography and make an overcast day seem sunny or a bright day appear shrouded in darkness. Similarly, we can change the symbols through which we perceive the world.

Psychologists have identified three symbols of death: disintegration, separation, and stasis. We can re-view these symbols and they can be used to open up our ways of thinking about the world. Once we become aware of our freedom in employing symbols, we recognize our freedom in how we react to the human condition. We will then explore the fundamental symbols of space, time, and love.

Space is a formative concept involved not only with our notions of distance and area, but with separation, otherness, connectedness, opening out, and enclosing. The biblical book of Jonah offers a powerful discussion of space, especially in terms of constriction (inside the whale) and opening out (to the people of Nineveh). We must also think about *otherness*, in all its aspects. We must discover what we identify as other, when we are inclined to judge something as being other, and how we may become one with the other.

Time is related to change, to meaning, to memory, and to faith. Time can be perceived as a burden, as it is in the biblical book of Ecclesiastes. The problem presented there is answered in the Song of Songs, which clarifies the role of time in the emotions and shows especially how love can transform our perception of time.

If love can transform our perception of time or space, it must in some sense be more fundamental than these two concepts. The centricity of love for enlivening and supporting our world is illustrated in the story of the *lamed-vovniks* of Jewish tradition — the thirty-six secret saints for whose sake the world is sustained. If the world is supported by so few and their loss threatens our life-giving world, we begin to recognize the importance of mourning. As we contemplate the special people inhabiting our personal world, we think about the whole notion of friendship. Friendship is shown to be a way of knowing and a way of creating.

Love and friendship also lie at the heart of the biblical message. If we examine the Ten Commandments, we discover the transformative process of love that helps us make our world come alive.

We must find ways to apply these thought-out symbols to re-envision our world. We explore ways of remembering who we are — of being faithful to an experience of aliveness. We recognize our relationship to those who have helped create our world, our shared perspectives, and our variant angles. We hope to make our contribution to a vision of this world. Above all, we recognize our role in shaping ourselves and our world by our choices of images and symbols.

1

Deadness in Life

Sometimes we feel that our world has been reduced to two dimensions and that we are missing the dimension of meaning. These are not times of fear or pain, because those sensations still entail meaning; even fear entails hope. But when the world is robbed of meaning, one outcome is as meaningless as the other; fear and pain have disappeared because we cannot feel at all.

When the world becomes flat for us we must search for a life principle, because flatness is death. We see this life principle in the startling independence of the being of another species — it just exists, grows, and persists. We find the principle in the affection of other people, in their concern, and even in their anger. We find it in the forces that pit themselves against us — the blinding rain, the sudden wind, the snappy cold.

The life principle is found in and through the ordinary, though when the taste for life has departed, we may sense it as extraordinary. When something obstructs our power to taste life, then ordinary delights can indeed be extraordinary. We try to recall what made us enjoy a setting, an activity, or the company of another person, but the life-giving power eludes us.

We have no sure defense against deadness. We can believe with perfect faith until that sudden day when we hardly remember why we once believed. We may love with absolute devotion until one day we cannot bear the presence of our beloved. We love the cat until it sits once too often on the page we are reading or meows just as we are dozing off. We find this world wondrous and suddenly it ceases to attract us. Our only defenses against the onslaught of deadness seem to be the tenacity of faith and the habits of attention we have built up.

In a context of deadness, isolation, and despair, we begin to think about our will to live when the will no longer seems natural. In the face of its impending or actual loss, we become conscious of it and wonder what it was and how we came to lose it.

Our lessening of vitality or the will to live can be characterized in many ways: deadness, dejection, melancholy, ennui, psychic numbing, dryness, listlessness, apathy of the soul, or depression. Each of these characterizations sheds some light on the question of who we are and how we are related to the rest of reality. We must not deny ourselves the experience of deadness but must take it as an indication of where we are in our world. Our emotions are significant and we deny them at our own risk. They are important resources for insights — for becoming conscious of our vision of reality.

THE DESERT FATHERS

The Desert Fathers were fourth-century monks who lived in Egypt, Arabia, and Palestine. They were removed from most worldly distractions and could give their emotions the kind of careful observation and analysis that would not be seen again until the Freudian era. They called the deadness we are examining *accidie* and recognized it as a temptation to abandon their commitments. Deadness, or *accidie*, was recognized as bringing on the trials of impatience, anger, hatred, contentiousness, and despair. In fact, it represents a breakdown of the system of meaning and value. By calling deadness a temptation and a trial, the Desert Fathers placed the personal experience of aridity within the larger context of a meaning system in which suffering is purposeful, valuable, and — ultimately — vindicated. Even though they were treating deadness as it occurred in people who were already sufficiently committed to a redemptive world view to live monastic lives, they found deadness to be corrosive and damaging. They thought deeply about it and developed some significant insights that will serve as our starting point to discuss deadness.

> When our soul begins to lose its appetite for earthly beauties, a spirit of listlessness is apt to steal into it. This prevents us from taking pleasure in study and teaching, and from feeling any strong desire for the blessings prepared for us in the life to come; it also leads us to disparage this transient life excessively, as not possessing anything of value.[1]

We see that even in the ascetic community of the Desert Fathers, a failure to recognize earthly beauty was regarded as fostering the temptation of deadness. Asceticism is not incompatible with joy, and the loss of our capacity for joy is the loss of our receptivity to ongoing revelation in and through the natural world. We must love this world even as we acknowledge that we should not try to possess it.

We can also draw a deeper message from the views of the Desert Fathers: our failure to appreciate this world somehow cuts us off from its life-giving capacities. We are a part of something, and our being and well-being requires our recognizing, sustaining, and deepening this connection.

7

Giving deadness significance by calling it a temptation, a trial, or a demon, placed it within the meaning system of the Desert Fathers and strengthened the resolution of the monks not to yield to it. Since deadness is characterized by a breakdown of meaning and value, placing it within a meaning system helps in overcoming it. But calling deadness a temptation does not illuminate its causes and may keep us from seeking such causes. The Desert Father Evagrios the Solitary recognized this problem and went beyond merely ascribing labels to draw out some significant relationships.

> A monk should always act as if he was going to die tomorrow; yet he should treat his body as if it was going to live for many years. The first cuts off the inclination to listlessness, and makes the monk more diligent; the second keeps his body sound and his self-control well balanced.[2]

Evagrios points to a relationship between listlessness and time. The thought of the ongoingness of time can be burdensome, while the thought of an end of time can freshen our experience. While Evagrios draws our attention to an important connection, his solution has troubling implications. It might mean that we can enjoy something only if we hold in consciousness the thought of its impending loss. Are we incapable of enjoying something that persists? We will examine the relationship between deadness and the consciousness of time in chapter 4.

Evagrios offers a profound solution for deadness that was to find its best known application in the *Proslogion* of Saint Anselm and was later to become the heart of Spinoza's philosophy:

> If a certain listlessness overtakes us as a result of our efforts, we should climb a little up the rock of spiritual knowledge and play on the harp, plucking the strings with the skills

of such knowledge. Let us pasture our sheep below Mount Sinai, so that the God of our fathers may speak to us, too, out of the bush and show us the inner essence of signs and wonders.[3]

Evagrios is here attempting to heal one of the greatest of human conflicts — the separation between head and heart, or reason and the emotions. He suggests that our intellect can be employed in the service of our emotions. Spinoza makes precisely the same point in observing that negative emotions can be overcome only through the strongest of all emotions, the intellectual love of God.[4]

THE ONTOLOGICAL ARGUMENT

Anselm's application of this insight is found in what became known as the Ontological Argument for the Existence of God. In it Anselm asserts that the very idea of God necessitates God's existence. Just as there are things we can rule out of existence once we understand their essence (square circles, for example), Anselm argues that God's essence forces us to recognize that God necessarily exists.

The ontological argument has fascinated people for centuries, though it has probably been as much misunderstood as it has been valued. Before we can judge whether a statement answers a question, we must understand the question. The ontological argument has been regarded for centuries as a "proof" for the existence of God, but that interpretation ignores the context within which it was formulated. Anselm, Abbot of Bec, was writing the *Proslogion* in 1078 for the benefit of his fellow monks, so the ontological argument was addressed to a community of believers and was never meant to convince the doubter. It was written as an aid to overcoming spiritual aridity and deadness.

The ontological argument should not be taken on a speculative or theological level, but on an experiential level. It was Anselm's response to what was, in effect, an emotional problem — loss of joy in life. In a period of spiritual desolation, the world does not speak to us. Using nothing but the idea of God, Anselm's argument seeks to renew us and reaffirm to us the value of our commitments. "To seek God becomes a metaphor for a life that has a shape and a direction, although not an agenda."[5] Anselm's search for God was one with his plea for assurance that his commitments were of value. *Accidie* attacks our commitments, connections, relationships, and practices. Anselm's concern is ours as well — that our day-to-day life is serious and significant.

The ontological argument is important because it gives us a context within which to lift up our deadness and view it in a new perspective. Our minds may remember that life was once sweet, that we were deeply engaged in it, and that we felt real commitment, but our emotions have "forgotten." We experience a radical split between head and heart, and the despondency of the heart is more forceful. The ontological argument appeals to the rational and appears to engage the intellect, but experientially, while the mind is engaged with the argument, the heart is lifted up. The split heals and the deadness, for the time, is vanquished.

It is important to stress "for the time." We cannot once and forever conquer deadness and despair, but we can come to understand when it comes, how it responds to busyness or stillness, and what we can do to transform the context in which it occurs. *Accidie* attacks our practices — it afflicts the deeply religious in their daily repetition of prayers, and it afflicts nonbelievers in their daily routines. Our practices are vulnerable just because they are habitual. We can brace ourselves for one heroic stance, but our day-to-day obligations can overcome us unless we discover a way to keep alive the wonder, the awe, and the sense of sanctity in our ordinary lives.

Evagrios suggests that the route out of *accidie* is the road to Sinai. That is the road Anselm uses, focusing on the name of God; and it is the road used by the twentieth-century theologian Abraham Joshua Heschel, who also stresses the power of the name:

> To name Him is a risk, a forcing of the consciousness beyond itself. To refer to Him, means almost to get outside oneself.[6]

The treatment suggests the cause: if the cure is to get outside oneself, then the cause may be the closing in on oneself. When we become locked in and closed off from others, we lose our connection to life-giving forces.

> Listlessness is an apathy of soul; and a soul becomes apathetic when sick with self-indulgence.[7]

Let us examine how Anselm's argument actually works, now that we recognize that it is not a proof. His first chapter, titled "A Rousing of the Mind to the Contemplation of God," begins:

> Come now, insignificant man, fly for a moment from your affairs, escape for a little while from the tumult of your thoughts. Put aside now your weighty cares and leave your wearisome toils. Abandon yourself for a little to God and rest for a little in Him. Enter into the inner chamber of your soul, shut out everything save God and what can be of help in your quest for Him and having locked the door seek Him out. Speak now, my whole heart, speak now to God: "I seek Your countenance, O Lord, Your countenance I seek."[8]

11

Anselm begins with a call to a deep stillness and a quest for God — not for the *idea* of God, but for the *experience* of God. Asserting that God does or does not exist is not meaningful until we have defined God. The term "God" is merely a cliché unless the name is rooted in the deepest experiences of our being. Anselm tries to move us toward a deep stillness, out of whose depth words can bring forth real meaning. We are not seeking a conventional or normative use of the term, but a use rooted in personal experience. The word "God" challenges us to respond with an answering echo of a time and a place when "God" referred to something we knew. If we were once enlivened by the thought "God" and our spirits quickened, then we have experienced divinity. Now in our listlessness we attempt to relocate the empowering center of our lives.

If we are unable to locate God in our memory, Anselm provides us with a definition to challenge us and to lift us out of our despair: God is "something than which nothing greater can be thought." Each of those words can be viewed as a rung on a ladder across an abyss. Our minds get caught up with the formulation, "than which nothing greater can be thought." We try to stretch our minds, refusing to acknowledge their limits, but as far as we can push our thoughts we find them enclosed within the encompassing protection, God:

> If I ascend to heaven, You are there; if I descend to Sheol, You are there too. (Ps. 139:8)

Anselm's "proof"[9] takes the form of a rational argument, a *reductio ad absurdum*, with the following structure: (1) God exists in the understanding but not in reality (proposition to be disproved); (2) God is something than which nothing greater can be thought (definition); (3) existence in reality is greater than existence in the understanding alone (first premise); (4) something that possesses all of God's properties as well as existence in reality can be thought (second premise); (5) something that possesses all of God's properties as well as existence is greater than God (1 and 3 combined); (6) something greater than God can be thought (4 and 5 combined); (7) it is false that something greater than God can be thought (2); and (8) it is false that God exists in the understanding but not in reality.

All the literature on the ontological argument (this writer's doctoral dissertation included) treats it as a strictly rational exercise. But if we explore what is happening within and to us as we are engaged with the argument, we discover that the ontological argument accomplishes more than this structure suggests. In attempting to understand the argument, we wrestle with an abstract concept, "something than which nothing greater can be thought." It is an expansive notion that begins to take us beyond ourselves. We come to realize that the *process* of being engaged in the ontological argument is more productive of emotional change than the rationality of the argument could ever be. Put another way, Anselm's argument is structured logically but works on us psychologically. Our conscious mind does indeed employ a function that can heal us, but it cannot be understood in the narrow sense of rationality. The intellect in its role of gathering or retrieving facts cannot lift us out of despair. Only in its role of making and employing images or envisioning possibilities can the head come to the aid of the heart. So while we may say that reason or the intellect can lead the emotions out of despair, we would be omitting the most important step in the process.

Just as studying great photography may help us improve our own picture taking, studying images that inspire and empower may help us develop our own liberating images. In examining the force and power of images, we have looked at the writings of the Desert Fathers and at Anselm's ontological argument. Looking in the Jewish prayer book, we find a blessing to be recited on witnessing natural wonders, including great deserts. It begins with the usual formula, "Blessed art thou, Almighty our God, Ruler of the universe," and ends "who hast made the creation." Like Anselm's argument, the blessing can work as a brief formulation to overcome our own desert — the dryness, deadness, loneliness, and despair that we confront periodically throughout our lives. The first ten words, the same for most blessings, create the context within which the final five words can effect their liberation. "Blessed"— the word, implying peace, serenity, and wholeness — is too often dismissed. We must force ourselves to recover a time and an experience during which the word had meaning for us. "Almighty our God"— God is not *my* God alone, even as *accidie* locks me into myself. Reciting the blessing forces me back into community that acknowledges "our" God. "Ruler of the universe"— at a time when meaning has broken down, we reaffirm that all of creation is under God's care and design; that it constitutes a whole, a oneness, a universe even in the face of the seeming chaos of the wilderness. The final five words, "who hast made the creation," may lead us to ask why, in the sterile and barren desert, we should focus on creation. The answer is that creation is the antidote to deadness. When we see creatively — see life and light, meaning and form — we move beyond the desert.

THE HASIDIC TRADITION

The responses to deadness offered both by the ontological argument and the Jewish prayer book are ad-

14

dressed to the faithful. We do not — indeed cannot — always have faith, but our loss of faith can itself be enclosed within a larger meaning system. The writer Isaac Bashevis Singer expresses this idea poignantly:

> Men are the children of the Highest, and the Almighty plays hide and seek with them. He hides his face, and the children seek him while they have faith that He exists. But what if, God forbid, one loses faith? The wicked live on denials; denials in themselves are also a faith, faith in evil-doing, and from it one can draw strength for the body. But if the pious man loses his faith, the truth is shown to him, and he is recalled. This is the symbolic meaning of the words, "When a man dies in a tent": when the pious man falls from his rank, and becomes, like the wicked, without permanent shelter, then a light shines from above, and all doubts cease.[10]

In the story, the Hasidic Rabbi Bainish of Komarov had buried his third son and had stopped praying for his ailing children. When his youngest daughter also died, he did not even follow her hearse. All that he had believed now seemed to him false, though he contributed ever-increasing amounts to charity. Eventually he sees a vision of his youngest daughter, after which he seems to return to his former self. Then he lies down on his deathbed and sees visions of his four sons, his two daughters, his father, and his grandfather, all reaching out to him. His final words are, "One should always be joyous."

The joy of Singer's story is compatible with deep grief and loss. Great religious teachers have understood that "negative" states, such as melancholy, doubt, and pain, form an integral part of a life of faith. "God is everywhere, said the Besht [Rabbi Israel Baal Shem Tov]. In pain too? Yes, in pain too — especially in pain."[11] The joy described in Elie Wiesel's study of four Hasidic masters, however, is at odds with melancholy. The struggle against melancholy and pain ultimately defeats the four mas-

15

ters. They repressed their personal pain in order to inspire joy in their followers, but they did so at great cost to their own well-being. Each one's life ended in anguish and defeat, in part because he did not allow himself to experience pain as a legitimate part of his faith. But they taught their followers that they must place their sorrow and despair within a larger context of an eternal relationship to God, whether or not they experienced God's presence:

> Often students would turn to [Rabbi Pinhas of Koretz] for help in matters of faith. To one he said: "True, God may be hiding, but you know it. That ought to be sufficient." Will the student suffer less? No, he will suffer differently.[12]

That difference is an essential one. Meaningful suffering — suffering that occurs in the context of faith — is experienced in a radically different way from meaningless suffering. The masters recognized the proximity of faith to deadness:

> Look in front of you. Look beyond that gate. What keeps man from running, dashing over its threshold? What keeps man from falling? Faith. Yes, son: beyond the fiftieth gate there is not only the abyss but also faith — and they are one next to the other.[13]

The Hasidic masters "addressed themselves to forlorn and forsaken villagers . . . turning imagination into a vehicle to take them away from misfortune."[14]

> The beauty of Rebbe Barukh is that he could speak of faith not as opposed to anguish but as being part of it. "Faith and the abyss are next to one another," he told his disciple. "I would even say: one within the other. True faith lies beyond questions; true faith comes after it has been challenged."[15]

In the same spirit, the Book of Ecclesiastes finds its

rightful role in the sacred canon. Tradition has ascribed to Ecclesiastes the archetypal expression of *accidie*. But if we dwell on the text we find that a deep trust pervades the book. Ecclesiastes' dictum that there is a time to mourn carries within it the idea that mourning is transitory and cannot ultimately destroy the larger pattern of meaning. Acknowledging that there is a time to mourn also acknowledges the importance of our emotions. We must not repress our emotions in an effort to avoid melancholy, for two reasons. The first results from our awareness that emotions can give us important information. Pain points to something that is wrong and as such it is a valuable signal that we ignore only at our peril. Similarly, our melancholy, guilt, and dis-ease are important signals that something is wrong that deserves our attention. The second reason for not repressing our emotions to avoid melancholy is that the process cannot succeed. The fear of melancholy betokens an inadequate trust in joy. "Joy is deeper yet than sorrow."[16] It is so deep, indeed, that we need not clutch it. If we let it go and deadness comes, our conscious interest in deadness can be enlivening and eventually the joy will return.

The Desert Fathers distinguish between the sorrow that accords with God's will and the sorrow that does not, which is deemed "destructive of holy thoughts and spiritual knowledge."[17] Buber draws a similar distinction between a broken heart, "which prepares man for the service of God," and dejection, which "corrodes service."[18] These distinctions are analogous to one that has been drawn by psychologist Robert J. Lifton between animating guilt and static guilt:

> An animating relationship to guilt exists when one can derive from imagery of self-condemnation energy toward renewal and change. . . . The term static guilt is used here . . . to emphasize deadening immobilization of the self.[19]

All these writers emphasize that there is a task we are called upon to fulfill. Whether an emotion is positive or negative depends on its effect on our performance of the task. Lifton defines our service in terms of renewal and change; Buber sees the task as our unique contribution to the world; and the Desert Fathers identify their task to be a life of prayer, study, and devotion. But we are not the Desert Fathers, the monks in Anselm's monastery, or the devout Hasidim of Singer's story. We can be grateful for the clues offered by these earlier teachers, but the task remains for us to find our own enlivening approach to deadness.

A NEW CONCEPT OF GOD

All these writers use a notion of God. If we locate God as being in and through all our experiences and beyond what we can hope to experience, we find the thought of God to be conducive to openness and expansiveness. This idea of reality, as something progressively revealed to us throughout our experiences and ultimately inexhaustible, is what I mean by God.[20]

How this definition operates can be shown by an analogy to the process of how we come to know our own parents. In our early years, our parents' roles are very much like God's: creator, nurturer, and preserver of our being and well-being. When we are infants we do not know our parents at all. Gradually we come to distinguish them from everyone else. We even get to the point where we can envision them when they are not present and so come to long for them. But their sole identity is still as our parents.

As we grow older, we eventually come to know our parents as having identities that transcend those of sup-

18

pliers of our needs, and we realize that they even have needs of their own. We come to know them better not because we have more data, but because we have gained more of our own experiences. We begin to know our parents out of the knowledge that comes with these experiences. When, in time, we become parents ourselves, much that mystified us in our childhood becomes transparent. For example, we now understand that they formulated rules for us not out of despotism but out of concern. With each passing year our own lives reveal more and more of who are parents really are. It can easily take a lifetime to know our parents. It can easily take all of humanity's *shared* lifetimes to come to some idea of who God is, though the approach is the same. We know God not as an object, not even as an object of devotion; we know God only out of our personal subjectivity.

The God we knew at age five is not the God we knew at fifteen. The God we knew with the birth of our first child is not the God we knew in the depths of mourning. Each experience deepens our understanding. The difference between the fifteen-year-old's experience of God and our own is not one of conceptual sophistication or intelligence. A person of fifteen can be intellectually mature but cannot have had a lifetime of experiences. We are concerned here not with knowledge but with wisdom.

This approach to the idea of God is important for two reasons. First, we should not discuss what we do not know. Second, we must not reduce the most significant concept, God, to a cliché. We must use the concept with conscious awareness that it will become more significant as we grow older if we continue to refer our experiences to a meaning system grounded in our relationship to God. In a positive sense, this unfolding characterization helps make life an adventure, keeps us open to all that we experience, and challenges us to reflect on our experiences and their place in our larger world view. If we accept this characterization, we can also observe that too many partial notions of God have been put forward as total notions. Ideas of God formulated from partial experience of, say, triumph ("The Lord, the Warrior" [Exod. 15:3]) or defeat ("God of retribution, Lord, God of retribution, appear! [Ps. 94:1]) are necessarily partial. Partial characterizations distort our idea of God and may cause us to discount our own experience.

A New Concept of Worship

As our idea of God progressively develops, so does our idea of worship. In its earlier stages, worship is separate from all other activities and the notion of the sacred appears only in separation from the profane. Later the distinction can become less sharp. Life itself is seen to be sacred and the affirmation of life, or the capacity to endure, can become the most profound form of worship. Heschel expresses this idea compellingly:

> To be is to obey the commandment of creation. God's word is at stake in being. There is a cosmic piety in sheer being. What is endures as a response to a command.[21]

Life is holy, but even as we realize that, we see the force of deadness within ourselves. Because we recognize the essential holiness of life, we come to realize that we are not fully holy because we are not fully alive. As theologian Howard Thurman writes:

> It is good . . . to look at the dead places in ourselves, those things which we have watched die because there was no nourishment we were able to give, or because in our fear

of life we strangled them to death. To look at the dead places
in our lives and contemplate the awful vitality of a great
resurrection.[22]

We can take responsibility for the dead places in our
lives, but we still wonder why we allow ourselves to become unfeeling. Probably it is because the feelings we
did have were feelings of pain. We close ourselves off
to life when we perceive it to be the place of loss, guilt,
and suffering, rather than the place of comfort, joy, and
peace. Certain events that tend to bring on deadness occur often enough that religions have developed ways of
responding to them. One such event is the death of a
close relative. The loss is painful and frightening. It brings
us closer to our own death and may result in our striking a "devil's bargain" with death. We deaden ourselves
to the world, and since we are not really alive, we cannot have life taken away from us. Such deadness in life
has been described in Lifton's account of the survivor
syndrome. The more we value life, the more we fear that
it will be taken from us. So we mute our joys and numb
ourselves to life's wonder. We thereby hope that in our
colorlessness we will be camouflaged from death. We
are then doubly at risk when a loved one dies. We experience the pain of loss, the great empty space that was
once filled with love, and we experience the fear of our
own death.

THE JEWISH MOURNER'S KADDISH

In the Jewish tradition, the risk is dealt with through
the daily recital, for eleven months after the death of
an immediate family member, of the Mourner's *Kaddish*. The prayer itself makes no reference to death — it

is concerned solely with the glorification of God. "Precisely at the moment when it is hardest so to do, we lift up our voice to assert the essential holiness and goodness of the Infinite":[23]

> Glorified and sanctified be God's great name throughout the world which thou hast created according to thy will. May God establish sovereignty in your lifetime and during your days, and within the life of the entire house of Israel, speedily and soon; and say, Amen.
> May God's great name be blessed forever and to all eternity. Blessed and praised, glorified and exalted, extolled and honored, adored and lauded be the name of the blessed Holy One, beyond all the blessings and hymns, praises and consolations that are ever spoken in the world; and say, Amen.
> May there be abundant peace from heaven, and life, for us and for all Israel; and say, Amen.
> May God who creates peace in the celestial heights create peace for us and for all Israel; and say, Amen.[24]

We may wonder how this prayer helps us overcome our pain, our fear, and our inner turmoil. Just when we are most turned in upon ourselves, we are forced to open up to the world created according to God's will. Just when we are self-absorbed in our grief, we are made to pray for an entire people. At the moment that we are bereft in time, we are made to focus on eternity. When we are most aware of the poverty of language to express our loss, we are reminded that while our grief is beyond language, so is the greatness of God. Beyond our anger and our rebellion against this judgment of death comes our prayer for peace. We cannot live as rebels; we must finally seek reconciliation with life, so we rejoin society in our prayer for peace. Heschel points out that

> faith is the fruit of hard, constant care and vigilance, of insistence upon remaining true to a vision; not an act of

inertia but an aspiration to maintain our responsiveness to [God] alive.[25]

Before our loved one died, we knew the goodness of the world and the many gifts of creation. Our task is to remember, even in pain and fear, what we once knew and where we once felt the presence. The Mourner's *Kaddish* goads our memory. The habit of reciting it daily creates a stable character of attention.

We have losses that are not so overt and for which the community does not come forward to aid us in facing the dead places in ourselves. We can lose, for example, our sense of dedication, of direction, of purpose, or of meaning. "Mid-way in the journey of our life, I came to myself in a dark wood where the straight way was lost."[26] This coming to ourselves can be frightening. The courage needed to face what we have become and what we have left behind may seem more than we can achieve. "Our greatest problem is not how to continue but how to return. . . . The deepest wisdom [we] can attain is to know that [our] destiny is to aid, to serve."[27]

2

Experience

I f we are to overcome deadness, we must each find our own enlivening approach. Our starting point in this task will be our own perceived experiences. To understand why experience is important, let us look for a moment at the world of prayer. Prayer consists of words, but its real meaning lies in the intention and focus behind the words. Heschel distinguishes between the words of a prayer and its *kavanah*, or inner devotion:

> Prayer as a way of speaking is a way that leads nowhere. The text must never be more important than *kavanah*, than inner devotion. The life of prayer depends not so much upon loyalty to custom as upon inner participation; not so much upon the length as upon the depth of the service.[1]

There is an inner reality not only to the life of prayer but — by extension — to all of life. We have a tendency to view ourselves only as objects and to view the world as a collection of objects. But we are much more than what we do; we consist also of an inner aspect that includes, for example, our intentions, our fears, and our expectations. If we can begin from within our own subjectivity, we will also be able to view the world as subject. As we examine our own experiences, we discover we know what *accidie* is, not from reading about it, but from having lived through it.

Accidie can be described behaviorally, but the heart of its meaning lies in its experienced sense. *Accidie* occurs when there is a split between the head and the heart. Intellectually we may remember that the world was once inviting, but the emotions no longer respond to the call. We have come to accept "knowledge" as a purely cognitive idea, ignoring its experiential aspect. But knowledge in its purely cognitive aspect cannot renew our commitment to the world. The knowledge that can must find its roots in our experience.

The world's major religious traditions show an awareness that our own experience is the touchstone of reality and value. The fifteenth-century neo-Confucian thinker Wang Yang-ming advocates that "experiential understanding of the classics through self-cultivation must take precedence over book learning."[2] In others words, we can come to understand a text by having lived through experiences analogous to those described in the text. Wang had been attracted to the Taoist way of self-cultivation and, indeed, set out to live his life in terms of Taoist values, attempting to become a hermit. Eventually, he realized that his filial feelings were so deeply rooted in his nature that to ignore them would be to deny the very foundation of his humanity. He then understood for the first time that his basic human feelings were the true foundation of his own self-realization.[3]

Thomas Merton, the twentieth-century Trappist monk, translated religious writings of Chuang Tzu. Merton's capacity to present these texts comes not from a strong linguistic base but from a shared experiential base:

> I think I may be pardoned for consorting with a Chinese recluse who shares the climate and peace of my own kind of solitude, and who is my own kind of person.[4]

Trusting our experiences may help us understand great texts, but its importance to our lives has a much more

compelling reason. We cannot achieve self-realization
if we ignore or mutilate the experiential part of the self.
Through our basic human feelings we can discover our
own basic values. If our emotions and experiences are
being distorted, then we must examine the conceptual/
ethical/religious system that distorts them. This position
lies at the heart of Wang's philosophy.

However, experiences alone are not sufficient to transform the self — we must have insight into our experiences.
Surprisingly, we are not always conscious of our feelings.
Sometimes we must deliberately notice moments of joy
and thereby learn when we are most whole and most
at peace. Psychoanalyst Joanna Field uses this approach
in her search for the experience of living.[5] Without pre-
judging what *should* make her happy, she records, over
a seven-year period, what in fact *does* make her happy.
As she records her experiences, she begins to explore
them: What is she doing when she feels happiness?
What is she thinking? Is there a quality of consciousness
or awareness that is consistently associated with her moments of happiness? Could this consciousness be developed and extended so that she can be happy more often
than not?

ENLIGHTENMENT

When we seek to understand Buddha's enlightenment,
we find that experience plays a central role. Enlightenment is liberation — not from prison or servitude — but
from our own bondage. While other traditions may char-
acterize this bondage differently, Buddha identifies the
enslaver as our own desiring. According to Buddha, we
cannot be at peace in this world because of the constant
burning of desire.

Describing Buddha as enlightened is not saying that he knew everything. We could rather say that he knew the one thing necessary for living a fully human life. This knowledge was not in the form of a possession of facts, but in a genuine transformation of being. Buddha had initially chosen the familiar approaches to enlightenment — going off to the wilderness and practicing extreme physical austerities — and found them lacking. According to tradition, he achieved enlightenment only after he abandoned asceticism, though we might already recognize an enlightening influence in his decision to leave the ascetic way.

When Buddha found that fasting and vigils had not made him enlightened, he sought another means of becoming whole and compassionate. His enlightenment consisted of his insight in trusting his own experiences. Teachers can offer paths, but we must finally test these paths by seeing if they do, in fact, help us become whole. Our path to wholeness cannot follow a formula. We constantly learn from others, but we adopt and adapt their teachings in the light of our own experience.

Were we to seek our own wholeness, we would search not in some esoteric practices but in our own memory. When did we feel natural and at one with all that surrounded us? When did we cease to struggle and feel peace? When did love, openness, joy, and warmth spontaneously flow from us? What were we doing at the time? Buddha's search is not very different from Joanna Field's, and both arrive at Socrates' dictum, "know thyself." All are agreed that reflecting on experience leads to enlightenment.

Why is Buddha's enlightenment so rare, Joanna Field's book such a revelation? Because from earliest childhood we are taught not to listen to our own impulses, but rather to some external authority. The call to obey external authority derives from a lack of faith in an inner authority. While their reasons are not always spelled out, those who emphasize external authority suspect that our inner nature is chaotic and not to be trusted.

What does it really mean to know ourselves? It means to be aware of our feelings — to value them and use them as a touchstone for behavior. This form of self-knowledge is what Socrates called his *daimon*. It means to recognize our uniqueness, which grows out of our different experiences, perspectives, strengths, and weaknesses, and to base our unique contribution on our unique identity. To know our self is, above all, not simply a mode of thinking but a mode of being — authentic being — rooted in the experiential. So while we must pay attention to some external authority, we must also heed our inner voice, trust in our own emotions, and avoid self-estrangement.

Our sensitivity to our own feelings leads to compassion. Why does this follow from self-awareness? When we meet a person *externally*, we are meeting an *object*, a surface. But when we meet someone from within our own experience, we meet a subject and an inner life. We come to know a sick person, a mourner, an insecure person, a frightened person, a lonely person, a caring person, or a joyous person not by observing behavior but by living through these experiences and so knowing from within the reality of these states. The external surface may be totally at odds with the inner turmoil.

The thought of meeting a person from within our own experiences is frightening unless we have achieved compassion for ourselves and for our weaknesses. Only when we have come to recognize our own neediness can we feel compassion for someone else's. Prior to that we may feel pity, but not compassion. In recognizing our own insufficiency, our need for others, we come to the aspect of ourselves that is both frightening and universal, but the universality helps us triumph over the fear. When Buddha saw the sick person, the old person, and the corpse and was able to say of them, that is I, he discovered both the cause of terror and the cure. In all that is living we see the cycle of growth, disintegration, aging, and death. This recognition, in the other, that what we are seeing is our own life cycle, is a form of love because we are meeting the other at a point that is deeper than our own coming to be and passing away. Compassion is what can overcome fear, but we can achieve compassion only by knowing ourselves.

We must go from the picture we wish to present to the world to the lived experience. We must know ourselves not as objects but from within our own subjectivity. And it is from this self-knowledge that we become able to know others. In Thurman's words,

> We live *inside* all experience, but we are permitted to bear witness only to the *outside*. Such is the riddle of life and the story of the passing of our days.[6]

Our World View

The further we push back our experiences, the more clearly we will see that we do not have "raw" experiences. Our experiences are always mediated to us by symbols. Stated as baldly as possible: we don't think in things. We think in symbols that represent things. When we think "a forty-pound rock" we may think in words, or visual images, or even in terms of a certain strain in our muscles. These symbols are not merely substitutes for objects; they are powerful tools for shaping our reaction and relation to reality. What are these symbols, where do they come from, and how do they function?

Infants were once thought to be like blank tablets taking in the impressions of the world. In effect, all an infant can do is digest. But just as digestion is an active process transforming what is not us (lettuce and carrots) into what is us (hair and skin and nails), so our perception is an active process transforming, through our unique contribution, some impulses into our experience. What is active in the infant is, in the adult, not only active but frequently conscious and deliberate. Regardless of physical limitations, we can determine our relationship to reality.

Marion Milner's words, "Without our own contribution we see nothing,"[7] locate very simply the essential place of our own freedom. The role of our own contribution in what we see and experience was vividly illustrated in a class I once taught in business ethics. The thirty students were employees of an insurance company. As the discussion went on, it became clear that although the students shared the same room, they did not inhabit the same world. Their own contributions were shaping what they in fact saw. For some the world was peopled by the dead as well as the living, and a sense of obligation extended to those who had come before. For others the world contained not only objects made up of matter and energy, but concepts such as truth, right, responsibility, justice. For some, their fellow employees were people from a particular ethnic, educational, and class background. For others, they were immortal souls carrying within them a divine spark. As we discussed cases — the moral dilemmas they had contributed from their daily work experience — it became apparent that their world views profoundly affected their experience of the dilemmas. Where some found a troubling moral dilemma, others found in the same situation a problem separate from all moral categories. Some regarded the

31

moral dilemmas of others as mere problems that a trained technician could solve without recourse to notions of obligation, value, or meaning.

Over the course of the months we worked together, we found that the "world we inhabited," our particular perspective, transformed our day-to-day experience. Our challenge was to learn to talk from our separate worlds, to communicate out of radically differing symbol systems. Ultimately we wanted not merely to communicate from our differing stances but to "try out" the different perspectives — to know, if only for a short time, what it would feel like to take a different world view seriously. The major tool that would enable us to enter into different world views was imagination.

IMAGINATION

If we are to develop moral sensitivity and awareness, we must develop our imagination. Imagination gives us our different world views, as my students discovered. Imagination can be a form of creative hope. Imaginative persons do not simply take reality as it comes to them — their hope transforms it. Dorothy Sayers comments that what the pagans in limbo could not imagine, they could not enter into.[8] Our world can be constricted by our vision of it. The capacity for the world to "baffle cynical prediction and offer wonderful surprises and transformations"[9] rests in part on our capacity to imagine.

Imagination's images are not simply powerful metaphors for thinking about our relationship to reality, although they are at least that. They are the places in which and through which we live. Our experience of value and meaning depends on our having images that allow us to rise above our world and gain a perspective on it. Some perspectives give us visions of despair and some, like Thurman's, give us visions of salvation transforming the lives that enter into them:

> But the place where the imagination shows its greatest powers as the *angelos*, the messenger, of God is in the miracle which it creates when one man, standing in his place, is able, while remaining there, to put himself in another man's place.[10]

So, finally, imagination can be a form of knowledge when it allows us to enter into the position of another person and so come to understand that person.

SYMBOLS

We seek to bring the tools of imagination to bear on the powerful force of symbols. Symbolizing begins in earliest childhood and perhaps before the acquisition of language. Thus the physical sensation of warmth comes to symbolize not only the lack of cold but safety, security, or even home. The earliest pre-linguistic symbols collect around them a constellation of images, sensations, and finally concepts, as the symbols grow along with us. An unused symbol may retain its childhood form and later be inadequate for our needs when as adults we reach back for it.

For example, suppose our symbol of God was formed, as it frequently is, between the ages of four and six. It contains aspects of a nurturing parent and aspects of a judgmental one as well. It comforts us when the lights go out, just as a parent would. When we are older we may formally study theology or the Bible, though we might not connect the studies with our own private image of God. The image is not re-examined. Life goes on. Then suddenly, as an adult, we are forced to look once again at the image, either because we face a life situation which leads us to want to call upon God or because someone has challenged our beliefs in such a way that makes us want to discover what we do, in fact, believe. The image we recover is embarrassing, like the worn teddy bear or the blanket we used to help ease our fears. If we have courage, we will reform the image, allowing it to grow along with the rest of our self. All too often, we simply dismiss the *concept* as childish, rather than the image which mediates it to us.[11]

We will be examining symbols as they apply to death, literal death and the metaphoric "death in life" that threatens our self and our world. We will begin with the three symbols of death, developed by Robert J. Lifton, that grow out of the experience of the infant and can be developed into the world view of the thoughtful person: disintegration, separation, and stasis. And we will see if we can envision a new response to these three symbols so that they need not be symbols of death but can be regarded as symbols of life.

3

Symbols of
Death and Life

When the world goes dead for us, when it ceases
to engage us and is no longer a place where we
can find joy, there are two areas in which we can make
changes: we can attempt to change the world, or we can
try to change ourselves. But something is inherently
wrong with this formulation, because it sets us over
against the world as if we could somehow disengage ourselves and find a perspective from which to view it.
Clearly we are in the world, and the more we come to
know ourselves, the more we recognize that the world
is also deeply within us, in our way of thinking, and in
our being. When we think, there are not two separate
things, our thought and the world. Our thought is part
of the world, and the world is transformed by our thinking about it.

We think with symbols, so our thinking *about* symbols is an important means for transforming reality. Reality is, then, partly our responsibility. The correct use
of language, the careful exploration of all the nuances
of a symbol, become sacred tasks as we try to be as clear,
open, and honest as we can become in our interactions
with reality.

In a powerful photo-essay called *Life at the Limits*, Walter Kaufmann shows people in India living in conditions of extreme poverty. He writes:

> Most of the people in these pictures do not look depressing because they are not depressed. They are destitute but do not respond to their condition in the stereotyped way that one might expect. It is widely supposed, even by philosophers, that the natural response to death is dread; to disaster and to destitution despair. But this is patently false, and this realization spells liberation. We are free to respond to what befalls us in any number of ways.[1]

What conditions the way we respond are the images and forms we bring to our experiences. The concepts we use to express the images, the anticipations, and the forms of thought we bring to experience are what I will mean by the term *symbols*. In effect, we will agree with both Susanne Langer's and Robert J. Lifton's position that we *construct* all of our experience "as the only means of perceiving, knowing, and feeling."[2] This construction is done by means of our symbols. Our first examination of symbols will be in terms of the symbols of death discovered and developed by Robert J. Lifton.

Disintegration

Lifton's first image of death is disintegration. We fall apart. The center will not hold, or there is no center. This image of disintegration is the reversal of the experience of "holding" in infancy. Holding is a complex process by which the nurturing parent helps the infant to become a self. It includes not only physical care (holding, warding off danger, minute adjustments to needs) but the holding in memory the many experiences of the infant that it cannot claim as its own. A self is being formed through perception, awareness, memory, and integration. This holding is embellished over a lifetime of experiences by things that reinforce our emerging sense of self: external validation, achievements, friends consonant with our values, and activities that center on our interests. All of these things which support our sense of self, our integrity, constitute elaboration of the initial symbol of holding. The opposite of this process is disintegration.

We have felt the horror of falling apart, of a lack of sense of self, of the fear that the center will not hold — or that there may be no center, no integrating pattern, no self. Montaigne even suggests that there is as much difference between us and ourselves as between us and others. Such an idea may indeed be a cause for optimism, but he offered it as evidence of our own inconsistency. We think we have certain unassailable principles, or characteristics, but we discover that the principles are not so unassailable, or that what we took to be essential characteristics faded with time. Who then are we? What persists through these many changes? Does anything endure? As the symbol for holding deepens and becomes embellished with our experience, so does the symbol for disintegration. The falling apart can be experienced physically, socially, psychologically, ethically, politically, or in other realms. All the senses of ourselves that contribute to our integration are areas in which we can experience disintegration.

What is it that really makes us ourselves? We may think it is our political beliefs. But if we move into another income bracket or marry into a family with different political views, we are no longer as certain. No one accompanies us into the voting booth, but some sense of our self has been subtly changed. Or the change can be less significant and more idiosyncratic. A college professor had to leave academia in order to find a job in business. Within a short time in the business community, he found that his pipe that had accompanied all his activities no longer pleased him. He had never thought of pipe smoking as constituting part of his image of an academic. He thought it was a habit that belonged to him and that helped, in a small way, define who he was. How much of what he did did he do out of genuine choice and pleasure, and how much out of some unconscious image of what a man in his position should be doing?

While our images of death are rooted in literal death, death itself has become the symbol for our deepest fears — of things falling apart, of ourselves falling apart, of disintegration. Can disintegration ever be creative?

Things do fall apart, but the result is not always destructive. Things can fall apart in order to regroup around a new center. We must "die" to one sense of our self in order to form a new sense of self. The process causes an upheaval. It is frightening. Is there any way to tell when disintegration is destructive and when it is creative; any way to tell when to marshall all of our resources against it and when to trust the process?

Part of the answer is social. Natural occasions in life entail some degree of disintegration. The movement from one social definition to another (child to youth, youth to adult, single person to married person, offspring to parent, married person to widow, etc.) will usually occasion fear of disintegration. "Expected" disintegration is not less frightening, but the social structure acknowledges it, supports it, and offers reassurance and sometimes structured guidance. We are certainly social creatures, but we are not simply social creatures living through and out of our social roles. We have our own concepts of ourselves, and any radical transformation of that concept can occasion disintegration.

Things happen to all of us that force us to redefine ourselves. Old age slows our once agile limbs so that our strength and energy no longer define us. When the re-definition comes with age, we may simply mourn for the self we are no more. But once in a while the loss of the old definition forces us to see its inadequacy. Our strength may be gone but we are not. Where is the defini-tion that touches on our essential self? The loss of the old definition becomes the quest for the real definition. The loss has become an invitation to a search, an adven-ture, an all-engrossing personal quest.

INTEGRATION

To get at the full force of the image of disintegration, let us explore the meaning of its life-giving opposite, in-tegration or integrity. We have approached it psycho-analytically in terms of the nurturing process of holding. Now let us explore it philosophically in terms of the con-cept of truth. What appears at first sight as an abstract, remote notion is, as we shall see, deeply rooted in ex-perience and rich in possibilities for our own thinking about renewal.

In mainstream twentieth-century Western thought, "truth" is defined as propositional truth, that is, the truth of a proposition or statement. This truth (called "noetic" truth) is dependent on a state of the world. For exam-ple, the statement "the chair is blue" is true if, in fact, there is a chair and it is blue. Now what do we do with the blue chair? In contemporary thought, nothing. But medieval thinkers were not afraid to examine what no-etic truth itself rested on. They discovered that noetic truth depended on there *being* a chair that was blue and they called *the being of this blue chair* "ontic" truth, or truth of being. It is in the realm of ontic truth that we locate integrity. Integrity has less to do with what we say than with who we are. Integrity has two characteristics: (1) being (as opposed to *not* being) and (2) being what you are (rather than being something else). There are many values implicit in these two characteristics. Being in the first sense is an achievement — enduring is something creditable. Being in the second sense entails the belief that we are in some sense unique and irreplaceable. Our job is to be us! But implied in that is a belief in meaning and value. Somehow it all makes sense, and we have a part to play in this meaning system.

We have seen that the philosophic system that gave rise to the notion of ontic truth began with the concept of noetic truth. We have also seen that noetic truth depends on ontic truth. We will now see that ontic truth, in turn, is dependent on Absolute truth, another concept that is avoided in twentieth-century discussions of truth. Absolute truth is, in religious thought, a name of God. It is what led Gandhi to call his autobiography *Experiments with Truth* and led Jesus to proclaim, "I am the way, the truth and the life."

While we are not accustomed to thinking in terms of ontic truth or integrity, it is not too difficult to do so because on some level it makes sense of our experience. We feel that being is an achievement we strive for and holding onto who we are, not being other, seems somehow more true. Absolute truth, the support of ontic truth, is a more difficult concept to assimilate. Belief in Absolute truth calls into question many of our assumptions, for example that truth is finally something human. Absolute truth holds that truth transcends our perspective on it. Truth has to do with reality as a whole. We are a part of that reality, and so partake of truth, but we are not the final arbiters of truth. As disconcerting as the acceptance of Absolute truth is to our everyday notion of truth, it is through Absolute truth that we find a response to disintegration. What allows us to disintegrate and not die? What allows us to let go of one sense of our self and still not fall apart but creatively reintegrate around a new center? What "holds" us after our nurturing parents no longer can? If our being and identity are the source of truth, we are like Atlas holding up the world. But if our being and identity are, in turn, upheld by Absolute truth, we can face disintegration with basic trust.

The theologian John Dunne writes about human truth:

> I can be crushed by my self-knowledge if there is no greater truth, no whole truth encompassing the truth I now know.[3]

This statement can be examined in terms of our three-fold notion of truth. As we come to know ourselves, and so know our imperfections, we can be overwhelmed if truth ends with us. If truth is human truth and human truth is inadequate, where can we turn? If wisdom is human wisdom and we have discovered the knowledge of our own ignorance, we will be crushed. But if we discover the knowledge of ignorance in a world whose truth is independent of our apprehending it, then we can accept that truth is not possessed but is worth striving for; we are imperfect but perfection is a standard; the world exists independently and truthfully. We view the world imperfectly but know that it is greater than our limited perception of it. Disintegration is terrifying when we are all that holds everything together. But in a world of Absolute truth, we can trust even as our own center shifts.

SEPARATION

The second image of death is separation. It is a powerful image rooted in the absolute dependency of infancy

41

but nourished and elaborated through all our losses. To be separated in infancy can literally mean to die. We need to be connected to our source of nourishment and protection. To be separated as an adult in some societies also entails literal death. For the nomad in a harsh environment, to be cut off from the rest of the people is to be unable to sustain life. When the Bible threatens that one who breaks a certain rule will be "cut off," it is not clear what this cutting off means. Tradition holds that cutting off means literal death, but an examination of the biblical world view suggests another interpretation. The world of the Bible is a world of faith. It is not a world of simple faith, but a world of testing, apostasy, return; it is a world grappling with faith. Death is real but not frightening. Abraham sees death not as "cutting off" but as gathering to his ancestors. Joseph can leap imaginatively beyond his own death to the ultimate liberation of his people and ask that his bones be carried out with them when they leave Egypt. Being cut off, then, is more frightening than death, even though the initial symbolism comes from death. To be cut off is to be divorced from meaning, continuity, and connectedness.

One of the peculiar things about separation is that even as it threatens life, it is absolutely essential for life. Our first separation is from our mother at birth. We must be expelled from a smaller world in order to enter into a larger one.

CONNECTION

In order to understand separation we should look at its life-giving opposite, connection. Biologist Lewis Thomas brings out the connectedness of life-forms:

We do not have solitary, isolated creatures. It is beyond our imagination to conceive of a single form of life that exists alone and independent, unattached to other forms. . . . Everything here is alive thanks to the living of everything else. All the forms of life are connected.[4]

We become conscious of connectedness and recognize another attribute that goes with it, concern. We are all here together, interdependent; so even apparent separation is in reality a new form of connection.

To think about connection is to think about community. One important sense of community is the community of pain. The pain can refer to the loss of a sense of ourselves, to a loss of confidence in our own well-being, or to the loss of a person we loved or a situation that pleased us. Pain occurs because we are only a part of a larger whole. In pain some conception of the larger whole forces itself on our consciousness either through opposing us or through relieving and sustaining us. Unfortunately there does not seem to be a similar community of joy. Sometimes joy, as an expansive notion, tends to foster a false sense of self-sufficiency. We are not self-sufficient, and all that we hold we hold in a most precarious way, but we are constantly guilty of self-deception. As the Buddhist analogy has it, we are all fighting in a marsh of quicksand. Those who realize it end their fighting at once. But in moments of joy, or in the absence of pain, we forget that the ground is sinking beneath our feet.

When we touch one another on the level of our shared awareness of pain and mortality, we touch something of infinite value. This is not to suggest that we should seek sorrow, but rather that we cannot escape it. If we do not recognize that no home exists where a loved one has not been lost, it is because we have failed to identify with our parents or with those around us.

43

But if everything is moving toward death (as in the quicksand analogy), everything is also moving toward life. Sometimes we can identify with this new growth, these new possibilities, this opening out of life. There is a deep pathos in the freshness of new life, because we see in it all its possibilities and recognize in it what was once young and tender in ourselves. But this recognition is taken up in the larger awareness, that of a life that is larger than each individual's participation in life.

TSIMTSUM

When is separation death, and when is it the prelude to fuller life? In Lurianic Kabbalah (a work of Jewish mysticism), creation is described as an act of divine contraction, *tsimtsum*. God contracts, thereby creating space for a created world. The mystics started with the view that God is all in all, or infinite (that outside of which there is nothing). They then raised the question of how there could be an independent world if God is everywhere. The spatial description is clearly metaphorical but it gives us a powerful image for thinking about God's voluntary self-limitation. God, in order to create an independent world, abandoned a region within God's self. But though the region is abandoned, God will return to it through creation and revelation. Of course we don't know whether God really contracted so that the world could appear. But we can use the doctrine to think of separation creatively, to envision uses for waning power, and to take seriously the idea that we are in the image of God, and we can recognize when contraction and withdrawal may be our greatest contribution.

It is hard to be a good gardener. Pruning plants, cutting back growth, and thinning flowers is troublesome.

44

We have difficulty because we project onto our plants the notion of individuality and then we are faced with the awesome judgment of who shall live and who shall die. We know that a branch is not an individual but rather a part of a whole. We also know that the well-being of the whole requires that we "pinch back" a branch that is robbing energy from the central line of growth. Yet standing before the branch we are brought up short. Will we ever think of ourselves not simply as individuals but as part of a whole? Will we ever recognize our need to cut short our own flowering so that the energy can flow to the central line of growth?

Only an extraordinary perspective could truly see the creative aspect of contraction, could accept it, and actually do it. Maybe that is why the mystics attributed contraction to God. It seems almost more than human to be able to achieve that vision. And yet it is offered to us as a vision of possibilities, a vision that there is a time to scale the heights and a time to encourage and applaud others as they, in turn, attempt to achieve.

Tsimtsum means contraction and restraining one form of our own growth. It also means seeing the creative possibilities in separation.

STASIS

Lifton's final image of death is stasis: the stillness, motionlessness, changelessness of death. How we hate to be restrained. Our very life and vitality seem to be connected to motion, energy, growth, and development. But not all stillness is death. Some of it is deep, quiet centeredness, a reaching down instead of a thrashing around. Nor is all motion rejuvenating; some motion dissipates. Thrashing about may even be a more accurate image of dying than stasis. The real distinction between the animate and the inanimate lies not in motion and stasis, but in the source of the motion. Inanimate objects move, but they are subject to necessity and inertia. Animate objects move through freedom and self-motivation. Self-motivation can create stillness or motion. An inaccurate focusing on motion rather than on the source of the motion may confuse us at times when the most rewarding thing we can do in our life is to be still.

Lifton's images of death (or what might better be described as counterimages of life) give us powerful symbols for exploring our own experiences of deadness. But we must not apply them or use them in a mechanical way. They are curiously ambiguous images. Looked at deeply enough we can see the image of death opening up into an image of deeper life. How then are we to understand or use them?

We cannot understand them as abstract images, separated from the life experiences that gave rise to and elaborated on them. We must bring them back to our own life, discover where they sound a deep chord of recognition or a discord of conflict. And we must discover whether the ambiguity may not, itself, be the richest and most powerful image of all; for while we know that "in the midst of life we are in death,"[5] our image may be hinting that death itself is the husk of a deeper, richer life.

4

Space

We have seen that the symbols we bring to our experience of the world radically transform our perception of the world. We have discovered that these symbols are wonderfully ambiguous, and in this recognition lies our freedom. But there are symbols more fundamental to our thinking — so fundamental, in fact, that we rarely think about them as symbols. Rather, we tend to take them as "given." The two fundamental symbols that operate in that way are space and time.

The Bible is silent about the creation of space and time. Both are givens within which creation occurs. But on the fourth day God creates the sun and moon to *mark* time. This marking of time (past, present, and future), called "perspective," presupposes spatial notions. As we order time, we think in terms of distant past or near future. Time also has a component that is non-spatial, called "duration," and this sense of time refers to time as *experienced* rather than as measured, ordered, or judged. Because of the conceptual priority of space, we will begin our discussion of the fundamental symbols space, time, and love with an examination of space.

There are many ways to think about space, ways that are themselves open to contradictory interpretation. Space can be understood as separation — an image that can be either isolating, estranging, and deadening, or creative, novel, and sacred. Space can be understood as enclosing or surrounding — an image that can be confining and constricting, or protective and embracing. Space gives rise to otherness and boundaries, and space gives rise to sameness and love.

OPENING OUT

The sky gives us two contrasting images for thinking about space. When we look at the sky on a clear night, we see bright stars, and beyond the bright stars we see dimmer stars, and still farther beyond those, dimmer stars. Our only limit is perception, not the vast resources of the universe. We get a true feeling of creatureliness, if creatureliness means insignificance, and the experience can be frightening. But on overcast days, the sky does not reach out into lonely space but comes close around us. There is a ceiling on our existence — a protective covering. The first view can feel overwhelming and impersonal. The second view can seem protective and sheltering. We need some way to go from what is close around us to what opens out without limit. Somehow the space that is personal, protective, and familiar must aid us in our transition to unlimited space. We need to recognize the aspect of space that touches us before leading us out to the vastness beyond ourselves. We begin with the familiar, but we are not restricted to that limited space. Reality need not be reduced to what touches and envelops, but that is where we begin. The two images of space are analogous to the two notions of God as impersonal and personal; the impersonal corresponds to the sense of vastness, while the personal corresponds to what is close and intimate.

We have many different associations with space. Some

are recalled, some are thought about, and some, almost kinetic, are felt in our muscles and limbs but are not available to us on a cognitive level. The Bible repeatedly demonstrates the many aspects of the symbol space.

The Book of Jonah gives us wonderful images for thinking about some of the central concepts of space by dealing with separation, otherness, enclosing, and opening out into. It represents an example of Giordano Bruno's statement, "Out of the universe we cannot fall." It is especially powerful in its treatment of space in terms of the image of the sky as constricting or enclosing.

The book begins with the call, "The word of the Lord came to Jonah." The call reveals two conflicting notions of place, which is space made personal. Place for Jonah represents his place in life, his style, his way of life, his community, and his location. All these are challenged when God calls Jonah to go to Nineveh. His place is then no longer a fixed way of life or location but a commitment that can transform all the other senses of place. Jonah must be made to realize that his place in life, the place of the righteous, is not for his sake but for the sake of what he is called upon to do in this world. Jonah attempts to flee the call by boarding a ship. The ship is soon struck by a tempest, but Jonah sleeps through it. His sleeping through his shipmates' cries of distress shows us what happens when we shut ourselves off from the call — we no longer recognize the needs we must address. We are called to fulfill a task in this world. Shutting ourselves off from the call is shutting ourselves off from the world.

Jonah tells the sailors to cast him overboard, a reaction consistent with his refusal of the call. He cuts himself off from his most essential aspect — the part that would answer his unique call. He cuts himself off from other people's aspirations as well and, in a final self-destructive move, he cuts himself off from life. Jonah's feeling, and ours in reading about Jonah, is one of absolute constriction. But the idea that we cannot fall out of the universe transforms the experience. There is no depth of despair to which we can fall, from which we cannot return. Jonah is swallowed by a fish that preserves his life and also enlivens him. His sleep during the tempest was the sleep of psychic numbing. He was dead to himself and to the suffering of others. When he finds himself in the fish, the suffering has at last become conscious. He experiences the constriction, remembers the truest aspect of himself — that there was work he was called upon to do — and so cries out to God and is released. The call is repeated, and this time Jonah is ready to answer it. He condemns Nineveh, Nineveh repents, God renounces the decree against Nineveh, and Jonah is disappointed. Once again Jonah is handicapped by a false notion of space. He feels he belongs in the place of the righteous, and he believes that Nineveh belongs in the place of the sinful. He has conceived an absolute boundary between self and other. His own experience of rejecting the call and being given a second call has failed to teach him compassion, the capacity to enter experientially the place of another.

If we perceive space as static, as the place we either occupy or fail to occupy, we risk the radical self-estrangement that afflicted Jonah when his place was changed. If we sense absolute boundaries between the self and the other, we experience alienation from others. We do need a standpoint from which to proceed, but place must be understood as a process rather than as a final position.

SPACE AND MEANING

Another image we have for thinking about space starts with our experiencing the world as three-dimensional.

When our world loses meaning and value, it becomes flat, or two-dimensional. The dimension of depth is the dimension of meaning. Depth can be experienced, for example, as perspective in painting, as the rich texture of polyphonic music, as the layers of time and subplot in literature, or as the organic interconnectedness in life. It is experienced visually, conceptually, tactually. When a rose is *merely* a rose — not a vibrantly living organism connected to all the rest of the world by roots, associations, and sensations — it becomes a two-dimensional rose, all make-believe. Meaning entails interconnectedness, just as place requires us to recognize the permeability of boundaries.

SPACE AND SEPARATION

Space implies separation: separation both as loss and as creative of opportunities. Stanley Keleman writes:

> Loss occurs . . . new space is created . . . the emotional reactions to loss and to space are experienced. New excitement is sensed . . . new possibilities are organized . . . new boundaries are formed.[1]

When separation is cutting ourselves off from our own deepest center, from others, and from the organic interconnectedness with others, it is deadening.

THE CREATION

The different ways of thinking about separation are illustrated in the first three chapters of Genesis. Creation on day one occurs through naming and separation. Our usual notion of separation is one of loss or cutting off and we forget its creative capacity. The account of creation through separation continues in Genesis on day two. God separates the waters above from the waters below, thus distinguishing Heaven from the Earth. On day three the separation of dry land from water allows the earth's fertility to emerge. Our first notions of space in Genesis are of an all-pervasive entity which must be separated, named, and kept in discrete areas. Separation is creative and good, but that goodness changes radically with the expulsion from Eden. Separation then becomes loss, and longing emerges. A space is created through separation, one that can be construed either as a void or as a plenum, and in that ambiguity of interpretation lies our freedom.

BIBLICAL AMBIVALENCE

After Genesis, the Bible is curiously ambivalent about space. It seems to be valuing space by holding out the goal of the "promised land." Yet two spaces that should be prime candidates for holiness, Mount Sinai and Moses' grave, do not achieve that status. Mount Sinai is never clearly identified nor is Moses' grave located. The sacredness of particular spaces is nowhere more forcefully negated than in Lamentations where, one by one, the spatial symbols such as city, wall, temple, and ramparts are destroyed but the faith endures. It does so because faith is not grounded in a holy *place* but in a holiness that transcends space. There are dangers in focusing on space or place, just as there are dangers in negating space or place. One danger in focusing on place, or "putting down roots," is that we embrace possessiveness, forgetting that it is God to whom all land ultimately belongs. Another danger is idolatry, or attributing holiness to something independent of its relationship to God. No land, finally, is uniquely holy. Holiness belongs to God, who is rightly called the Place of the World. But if "putting down roots" or excessive concern for a particular land is dangerous, nomadism has its pitfalls as well. We can dissipate energy by ceaseless wandering and we can withhold essential commitment. If we are on earth for the work we are to do, then we must enter deeply into this world, not pass through it lightly and uncaringly.

If we think of the Bible as demonstrating how faith is developed, then we understand better the Bible's ambivalence about space. Heschel clarifies this development:

> Originally the holy (*kadosh*) meant that which is set apart, isolated, segregated. In Jewish piety it assumed a new meaning, denoting a quality that is involved, immersed in common and earthly endeavors.[2]

The holy may be pointed out at first by contrast and distinction, but ultimately it must be perceived in and through all things. The process is analogous to that of children learning colors. At first, in order to teach children the meaning of "blue," we must separate blue objects from those that are not blue, or that are partially blue. Once the children have understood what is being focused on, they might well notice traces of blue in gray shadows or in green grass. The Bible is demonstrating that the holy is not other than the secular; rather, it is a different dimension of the secular. The waters above are not other than the waters below; what we take to be other is actually a different perspective on the same waters. The "other world" underlies, supports, and sustains this world and is perceivable in and through this world. Finally the Bible is at pains to teach us to perceive holiness in and through the secular, just as we are at pains to teach our children to perceive blue in all of

53

its subtle shading. We are trying to arouse and create a sensitivity.

> So, waiting, I have won from you the end: God's presence in each element. (Goethe)[3]

Space is concerned not only with separation and land but also with the sense of self, of otherness, and with the experience of diversity.

THE STORY OF BABEL

The importance of otherness and diversity seems to lie at the heart of the story of Babel. The traditional interpretation of events at the tower of Babel holds that the confusion of languages and subsequent dispersal of the population were a punishment for the people's sin. But when we search the text to discover what the "sin" actually was, we find that the text does not even mention sin, nor does it call the dispersal punishment. If we see the events not as a punishment but as God's correction of an incorrect action, we see that the people no longer speak one language and that they are required to spread out over the face of the earth. This corrective suggests that otherness is valuable. We should not be reduced to one language or one way of perceiving the world. This idea was already expressed in the fifteenth-century Torah commentary of Obadiah ben Jacob Sforno:

> The real crime of the builders was that they tried to impose one religion on mankind. God prevented this and, by dispersing the peoples, kept alive a variety of idolatries. But He knew that out of this diversity would eventually come a recognition of the Supreme Ruler.[4]

When we think about otherness, it is surprising that we can think of it only in terms of relationship. Something is not other, it is only other than something else and the very word used to ascribe distance actually affirms relationship. A mountain is not other than ourselves until we try to climb it and find our efforts pitted against its inflexibility. The breeze is not other than ourselves until it wafts over us, contrasting its coolness to our overheated condition. To look at otherness is to recognize our active role in the perception and to ask, who is the other? when is something other? why do we view it as other? and how do we become one with the other?

Otherness can refer to people, to styles of life, to material objects, to places, to states of being. Otherness changes: when we are young, adulthood is the other; gradually we take on the adult role and if we forget what it was to be young, then youth becomes the other.

DEATH

For most of our lives, death is the absolute other. But perhaps we will come to see that death is not something out there that comes to get us but, like adulthood, something we carry as a germ within us — something we gradually become. I tried to convey this idea some years ago in a fictional context:

> She thought of the cessation of her menses and the growth that did not squirm with life, the death she carried within her. Would she be ready to die, to leave with open heart and no regrets? Would she find death the final desert experience? She remembered when she first knew with certainty that she carried death, not life, within her. Each day now she took out the knowledge of her death and tried to explore it. Gradually the terrain was becoming familiar.[5]

Our sense of otherness is increased by fear. When we look at the changing nature of who is other, we realize that we ascribe otherness when we need to separate and blame. To take responsibility for our own aging and death is to gather them up as aspects of ourselves and not as other. We ascribe otherness when we are threatened, when we cannot deal with what has happened.

We need otherness, but we also need to recognize our connectedness. The problem of how to become one with the other is nowhere more vital than in our dealing with the notion of an other world. The major characteristic of the other world is that it is not this world. Yet there is a persistent strain in religious thought that suggests that the two worlds were once one and will again be one, and that we should contribute to unifying the worlds. If we can see the unity in otherness in some situations, we can begin to see how this world can be one with the other world.

THE OTHER WORLD

If this world is the temporal, the other world is eternal. But if we have never experienced the eternal, how can we attribute it to the other world? We do know the meaning of the eternal because we have experienced it in this world. As we examine the attributes of the other world — peace, justice, rest, presence of God — we find them imperfectly imaged in this world, just as we found adult status imperfectly imaged in our childhood. We gradually claimed this adulthood for ourselves and became one with the other. Similarly we may contribute to the task of bringing about a union between the two worlds.

Space

How can otherness be an entrance rather than a barrier? How can it help us discover the dimension of value in all we experience? Our usual mode of thinking is binary, that is, something is either A or not A. This is a convenient, shorthand way of thinking, but it can present problems. There are occasions when something is neither A nor not A, when it is not that sort of thing at all. For example, we may assume that something is either moral or immoral. But many decisions we make every day are simply outside the moral domain, such as our choice of toothpaste or of the color of our socks. The binary mode is especially dangerous in thinking about otherness, because otherness lies at the heart of some of our deepest prejudices. We think of ourselves as good, or at least as well-intentioned. When we recognize that someone is other than us, we may conclude that they are not good, or even that they are evil. Diversity, instead of being enriching, is perceived as a threat to our values. Nevertheless, otherness *is* other and any attempt to reduce or suppress difference goes against the diversity that lies at the heart of creation. How does otherness, then, lead us back to a vision of value? It does so by enlarging our perspective and showing us that it is *our* perspective. If other people see things differently from the way we do, we may not come to agree with them but at least we become aware that we have a perspective. Reality is larger than our awareness of it, which is why it can stretch us. This stretching is often uncomfortable, even frightening, so we prefer to spend time with people whose perception of reality agrees with ours. But we need to rub up against otherness and become open to the perspectives we have not yet explored. We

57

must become aware that we ourselves are practicing a variety of idolatry—we are believing that our partial and incomplete perception of reality is the whole truth. When we become aware of that belief, we break its hold over us. To know that we don't know is to be open — and otherness can become a way.

ALIVENESS

The way of otherness is the way of joy, where joy is the life force. We can see how otherness and aliveness are related if we look at their characteristics in common. What we find in both is something that doesn't do exactly what we want, something that is independent of us and so can disappoint us, but also something that can surprise and delight us. Because it is other it can refresh us.

Watering plants is either a task or it is a moment of communion with another aspect of creation, an aspect that is alive and other. We sense aliveness in the new shoot that sprang up when we weren't attending; we sense otherness in the strange weed that found itself in the pot. Should we let the weed grow and allow ourselves to discover what it is, or should we remove it now? We sense otherness in the damage done by our neglect. We cannot water a plant once for all time. In the week when we were too preoccupied to tend the plants, they were silent but were still in need. Now the collapsed leaves demonstrate that, unlike a book that can be put on the shelf and turned to later with no harm done, that which is alive forces itself into our consciousness.

Our plants are silent, our pets are not, but we can meet both their needs without nourishing our awareness. We can walk our pets thoughtlessly and leave them food without taking time to notice their presence. Our friends at a distance are sometimes as silent as plants. That does not mean our neglect does them no harm; it means only that we are not as aware of the harm.

What is alive is other and independent, so it has the capacity to surprise us. If we are to be nourished from the mystery of another being, we must enter into a committed relationship. The dog we don't love cannot delight us. As we quietly move from pot to pot, watering our plants and breathing in the rich warm scent of moistened soil, we get some sense of the privilege of being part of the life cycle. We are conscious that a plant is alive and has its own life to live out. The wonder a plant opens to us by simply sharing its aliveness is compounded as we move to animals and becomes almost overwhelming when we come to people. That is not to say that we always like them, or that they are always cheerful and courteous. It is to say that each person is a profound mystery, and as we are reminded from time to time that we are in the presence of a mystery, we feel that sense of awe and excitement that enlivens us. People live out their lives and we may be part of their chain of nourishment. If so, we are likely to be nourished by having a place to give. They may be part of our chain, or we may meet them briefly in a chance encounter. If we meet them with the awareness that they have a destiny to fulfill even as we do, we will have reverence for them and their unknown mission and find the world around us ripe with meaning.

We meet our plants, the birds who come to our feeder, our pets, our family, our friends, and sometimes we meet ourselves. That significant occasion when we encounter ourselves allows us to recognize that we too are a mystery and a wonder of creation, with a destiny to fulfill.

How does the Bible teach us about aliveness and convince us that we are not the only beings alive in a dead setting? It does so by emphasizing the aliveness and otherness of God. Samuel Terrien writes that the Jews of the Bible "worshipped a God whose disclosure or proximity always had a certain quality of elusiveness."[6] Elusiveness entails otherness and aliveness. We can control a figment of our imagination, but we cannot control something that is alive. What is alive, independent, and other, turns up when we least expect it and sometimes it fails to turn up when we want it most anxiously. We may, from time to time, be disappointed by what is alive, but we would be deadened by something we could control perfectly. The aspects of freedom and surprise in our encounters with God lead us to relate to God the way we relate to another person. We try to be faithful to our commitments but we recognize that being faithful to liturgy will not have a magical effect. We do what is within our power to create the context for a relationship to God while recognizing and respecting the essential mystery of the Other. Terrien writes further:

> The cultivation and the transmission of the faith, with its inescapable discipline of articulate thinking and moral service, springs from the central element of biblical religion, which is the elusiveness of presence in the midst of liturgical fidelity.[7]

The very failure of the world to perform as we desire is our assurance that it is alive. While its otherness may threaten us, it is also the key to our overcoming loneliness. We cannot overcome loneliness with something inorganic, nor can we overcome it with something that replicates our self. We need the aliveness of otherness while we find a way to maintain the self in relationship to the other.

5
Time

The way we understand the world changes us and changes the world, too. The more fundamental the concept we transform, the more deeply the transformation will affect our relationship to the world. We have seen that space, one of the so-called "givens" within which we structure our life, is not as unambiguously "given" as we had first imagined. Another of these so-called givens is time. Changing our understanding of time can help us come alive again.

According to Aristotle, time is the measurement of the before and after.[1] As such, time is a function of change. But the concept of change requires a stable center against which to measure change, so time is also a function of that which persists through change. From our perspective, what persists through change is our identity. Time is furthermore the medium through which narrative proceeds, and narrative is what allows us to understand our life as the unfolding of a story. It gives rise to notions of the past and the future which can cause, perhaps, a sense of loss and longing or a sense of anticipation and hope. All the emotions, except for the basic sensations of pleasure and pain, are shaped by reference to time. Fear, for example, carries with it the notion of future harm; guilt, the notion of past wrongdoing; hope

61

anticipates an event yet to occur; despair grieves for an outcome that is irrevocable.

Yet time itself is shaped by our way of thinking about it. Even such fundamental notions as birth, growth, progress, generation, conservation, decay, and death are cultural notions and are viewed differently within different cultures. Even within our own society people disagree about when life begins or when it ends and when a person stops being a dependent child and reaches maturity.

Linear Time Gives Rise to Uniqueness

> . . . Once
> everything, only *once. Once* and no more. And we, too,
> *once*. Never again. But having
> been this *once*, even though only *once*:
> having been on earth does not seem revokable.
> (Rainer Maria Rilke)[2]

Rilke has drawn out the essential distinction between the time before we were and the time after we will no longer be. The position he presents lies at the heart of Western religion and philosophy, which centers on the notion of the individual. It contrasts sharply with the Eastern view, which rejects the linear view of time and the role of the unique, irreplaceable individual. Rilke responds to the problem of death in terms of some real change we have made in this world. In the Eastern view, by contrast, a cyclical view of time leads to a view of death that is not absolute: as time reverses itself, so does death — we have been and we will be again. In that view, even the world itself has been, has ceased to be, has come into being again, and will cease to be again, in an ongoing process. The Talmud says,

A king of flesh and blood stamps his image on a coin, hence all coins look alike and are alike; but the King of Kings put the stamp of the first man on humanity, yet no man is like any other.[3]

What makes us unique individuals is, in part, that we do things which cannot be undone. Time makes a difference; change is real and has real consequences. If we do something with negative consequences, we cannot undo it (although we might make reparation). We experience guilt for what is past and cannot be changed. As we age we not only grow old, we have the opportunity to grow in wisdom. The characters in the Bible, too, are unique individuals. They are full-bodied people with definite tendencies, characteristics, and personalities. They age, and as they do, some of their youthful characteristics are tempered. The boastful Joseph of Genesis 37, who told his dreams to his brothers, is changed over the course of his years in slavery and prison, through reverses in fortune and the rescue of his family. Gone is his pride when his brothers fling themselves before him after the death of their father, and Joseph replies, "Have no fear! Am I a substitute for God? Besides, although you intended me harm, God intended it for good" (Gen. 50:19–20).

The story of Joseph's father, Jacob, is no less an example of the fine tempering of age. When we meet Jacob (Genesis 25ff.), he is a deceiver. He first deceives his brother Esau and later his blind father, Isaac. He flees to his uncle Laban in Haran and en route is given an awesome dream. But the vow that he makes as a result of the dream is not the product of faith and a life lived with God. Rather, it is the vow of an immature person who is only starting out on a life of faith.

If God remains with me, if He protects me on this journey that I am making, and gives me bread to eat and clothing to wear, and if I return safe to my father's house — the Lord shall be my God. (Gen. 28:20)

Jacob seeks to insure the future, but his notion of the future is shaped by his experience of the past. He cannot ask for protection for the two he will love most because he does not love them yet. Once in Haran he is deceived by his uncle. As time passes, he is deceived by his sons, experiencing in his own life the deception he had dealt Isaac. Just as he used the skin of a goat to deceive Isaac, his sons use the blood of a goat to deceive him. The mature, aged Jacob offers sacrifices to God before going down to Egypt. This time he does not ask for anything but listens to the last direct revelation God will offer mankind before the revelation to Moses:

> Fear not to go down to Egypt, for I will make you there into a great nation. I Myself will go down with you to Egypt, and I Myself will also bring you back; and Joseph's hand shall close your eyes. (Gen. 46:3)

Time has tempered Jacob, transforming him from a brash young man intent on his own goals to a wise man open to a perspective wider than that of his own individual needs.

Ongoingness of Time

One of the central problems of time in the Bible is that of its ongoingness. One heroic act does not last a lifetime. The next day dawns and we are called upon once again to do what is required of us, to be faithful to our commitments, to live, and to live well. The ongoingness of time really means that there will be no end of days and no end of the day's tasks. We cannot once and for all time overcome hatred, learn to love, be rid of loneliness. It also means that things do not become automatic or completed. We cannot brush our teeth once for all time. Marriage is not "automatic" after five, ten, fifteen, or even twenty-five years. We still need to say, "I love you," and still need to hear it said to us; we still need to work out our differences.

But while the day's tasks cannot be forever done, they can become easier. We begin to shape ourselves to our tasks and that is what it means to become faithful. Faithfulness refers to a practice, not a set of beliefs — it is manifested in the way we live our lives. We can have faith, for example, that exercise is healthy, but faithfulness requires that we actually *do* the exercise regularly. A dancer doing warmups may never skip them, but the accompanying strain eases through years of stretching the muscles. The task remains, but the person has been transformed and the task has become natural. Each time we overcome hatred, learn to love, or rid ourselves of loneliness, we "stretch our muscles" and the strain eases.

We have all experienced different, even contradictory characterizations of time, which suggests that time is none of these. We sense time rushing by one moment and hanging heavy on our hands the next. We see time bring a talent gracefully to fruition and we see it erode all talents and gifts. As we explore these opposing images, we realize that time itself is free of all characteristics but we project onto it our own bitterness, our sweetness, our anxiety, our restlessness.

The Book of Genesis brings out the difference between time as we experience it and time as we mark it as a people. The lesser lights — the sun, the moon, and the planets — are created to mark time. Their creation occurs after the creation of Light, which symbolizes the light of our consciousness. The implication is that our consciousness is prior to time and as such is not subject to time. By using the lesser lights to mark time, we allow some external motion to mark our internal processes and so we are joined into a community. Even though time remains an intensely private experience — whether nightmarish or joyous, leaden or mercurial — our private encounters are brought to common ground by our shared marking of time. Such marking of time is value-free and should not be confused with our symbolizing or interpretation of time. In that interpretation lie not only meaning and value but also freedom.

ONGOINGNESS MARKED BY RITUALS

> So long as the earth endures
> Seedtime and harvest,
> Cold and heat,
> Summer and winter,
> Day and night
> Shall not cease. (Gen. 8:22)

Just as God's covenant with Noah is for the ongoingness of time, so covenants in general are for ongoing relationships which require, on occasion, concrete expression. These "concrete expressions" I will call "rituals of relatedness." They are as varied as relationships themselves: cards, letters, telephone calls, greetings, special meals, special places, shared songs, hikes, jokes, glances.

We have rituals not only with other people but with something as abstract as time. Every morning we awaken and through rituals of relatedness reconnect ourselves to our world of meaning. For some, the day begins with a prayer on awakening:

> I give thanks unto thee, O Ruler who liveth and endureth, who hast mercifully restored my soul unto me; great is thy faithfulness.

We are restored not only into consciousness, but into a conceptual community — a meaning system. For others, the day begins with informal prayer: a quiet look around the room, still half in shadows, to see if the plants need watering, the cat's dish is filled, and the bird feeder needs to be restocked. As the shadows disperse, the birds will be coming to the feeder and it must be ready for them. For still others, morning brings the harsh invigorating transition from a warm dark bed to a cold forceful shower. As the rush of water returns energy and awareness to each part of the body, the restoration is to the self as bodied. Morning is a time of gathering up, of collecting — and these daily rituals serve as a time of recommitment.

Mystics have emphasized the value of different states of consciousness. However, most of us choose to value and give our attention to the form of consciousness we inhabit in common — our waking state. Sleep is a different state of consciousness, but because we have experienced it all our lives without special settings, unusual postures, or drugs, we don't find the transition to and from sleep significant. Yet these transitions are important for an understanding of our sense of self, our sense of trust, our experience of commitment, and our awareness and conscious choice of our story. The elaborate deformation and re-formation of meaning systems reported by mystics after their ecstasies are open to all of us. We have all experienced a reality beyond space and time in our daily transition to and from sleep. We could, in principle, re-form our own meaning system after experiencing the different reality of sleep, but we choose not to give such priority to the sleeping state.

During sleep we have experiences — dreams — and we have periods of nonexperience. We know we have dreams because often we remember them after we wake up.

Sometimes we remember only that we dreamed without recollecting the dreams themselves. We can infer the periods of nonexperience by calculating when we went to sleep and when we awoke. The calculation requires an external source, such as a clock or the position of the sun, or an internal source, such as our state of hunger. But neither our awareness nor our consciousness testifies to the time of our sleep. In the mystic view, going beyond space and time is a central achievement that allows for the form of symbolic immortality that Lifton calls "transcendence." Yet this supposed achievement is something we all experience nightly. Furthermore, we give it up every morning as we opt back into the world of time and space through our rituals of relatedness.

The notion that we choose to enter time and space and choose to be in a story is reflected in the biblical account of creation. The lights in the firmament are to divide the day from the night and to serve as signs for seasons, days, and years. When we look to the heavens we observe markers for time. Time is part of our meaning system and our rituals connecting us to time represent serious commitments. Because our view of time is deeply ambivalent, we must become more aware of our rituals of relatedness, more determinedly conscious of our connections and commitments, and more explicit about the nature of our story.

WEARINESS OF TIME

The rituals that once delighted us can grow stale, or formal, or faded. What was new and fresh and spontaneous can grow dusty and worn. One way of renewing the rituals is by turning ahead the clock or by turning it back, returning to an earlier time. Turning back the clock returns us to an earlier state of our awareness and consciousness. We see our beloved as we did before the warts were discovered, before the daily irritations mounted up. Turning the clock ahead is to see our beloved with the awareness that we have only one last day together. Suddenly the very warts are loved and the behavior that irritated us will all too soon be gone. "Renew our days": the prayer is a plea not to turn back the clock but to transform our relationship to the world.

In our society people have tried both motions of the clock. We have attempted to push it back—to return to a simpler time and to reject the insights and awareness of a later time. We have also pushed the clock ahead, giving rise to a frightening consciousness that at any moment we may be viewing our home for the last time.

So filling the bird feeder is an act of profound prayer and commitment. It is a return from the timelessness of sleep to the ongoingness of human life. There is value in the fact that the feeder cannot be filled once for all time, it must be refilled each day. Filling it is a commitment to the clock as it stands. The clock is not pushed back to a time when the wood was not yet weathered by harsh winters or discolored by bird droppings; it is not pushed ahead to a time to end all time. Feeding the birds is a commitment to the present and to process—the ongoingness of time.

TIME AND MEMORY

Time is related to memory, which is necessary if we are to have a sense of self and if we are to love and be faithful. Identity is formed around memory, though not just any memory. Identity forms around the memory of our hopes, our dreams, our aspirations—in short, around

69

our sense of meaning. If we forget our meaning, we can hardly be identified as the same person we had been before. One of the functions of ritual is to help us remember who we are. But who are we and how do we discover our essential identity? Our attempts to answer these questions help explain our concern for rituals of relatedness. We have certain aptitudes, talents, and potentialities, but we do not know who we are until we are in place. Alone we are not fully ourselves, for our self lies in relationship to other beings and objects. The color red has a certain wavelength and appears to us as red. But red juxtaposed with white appears to us as a different color from red juxtaposed with purple. I may think of myself as an orchestra conductor. If I find myself on an uninhabited island without other musicians, I don't cease to exist but my principal way of thinking about myself must change. If we remove an organ from a body and attempt to study it by itself without reference to its place in an organism, we will not fully understand it. Part of what it is to be that organ is to have a role to play in a larger system. Analogously, to study *ourselves* apart from our work, our commitments, our relationships, our history, our traditions, our total environment, is to get a partial and frequently distorted sense of *ourselves*. We are, among other things, our role in a complex network of relationships.

We have an essential relationship to the work we do, whether we are paid or unpaid. Our work is where we make our contribution, although work is not always synonymous with job. We have an essential relationship, as well, to the place where we have been set down — the century, the culture, the geographical location, all of which are part of our sense of self. Our essential relationships include the people to whom we are committed, those we choose and those who are thrust on us by virtue of kinship. The relationships are determined in part by history: that we are the child of our particular parents. We cannot understand who we are without understanding that relationship. What we do with the facts of our parentage is part of our freedom and creativity, but the facts themselves are part of the raw material of our identity. We have a relationship to a tradition, one we may accept, reject, or modify, but one against which we must test the other ideas we hold. This tradition is not universal — it is as parochial as language and just as intimate. In what ways would we be different if we had grown up speaking Tibetan rather than English and if we had wrestled with a tradition of Tibetan Buddhism rather than Judaism or Christianity?

Many of our relationships are given to us by virtue of birth into a family, a culture, a nation, or a century. But we are also given the freedom to choose relationships. We emphasize some, neglect others, and create altogether new ones, and these relationships constitute our identity. We not only choose relationships, we choose styles of relationships: dominant, reciprocal, loyal, capricious.

Memory, like our relationships, is part of our identity, and memory is the source and sustainer of faith.

FAITH

When we think about faith, we think about trust and security. But there is nothing simple about faith. Faith brings not only trust, but doubts and uneasiness. Terrien suggests that one way to be true to this ambiguity and still transcend it is to focus on faith not as belief but as practice.

> The verb *he'emin*, "to have faith," . . . suggest[s] solidity and firmness not only in the realm of space but also in that

of time; hence it indicates durability, reliability, and endurance. . . . This is not an intellectual assent to a propositional truth. It is the insertion of the wholeness of one's personality into a relation of total openness toward the reality of God.[4]

Drawing on the idea of faith as practice, we can arrive at a definition of faith as an experience held in memory that becomes a warrant for hope. By this definition we have all had moments of revelation, that is, of knowing who we most really are. To some these moments are dismissed as the enthusiasm of childhood, as an aberration, or as a misjudgment. To others these moments are the most real moments of life, revealing the nature of existence. The memories of these experiences become the building blocks for a whole style of life. Heschel has expressed this idea:

> God's grace resounds in our lives like a staccato. Only by retaining the seemingly disconnected notes comes the ability to grasp the theme.[5]

Because faith is based on an experience, it requires faithfulness — that is, believing in our own experience, holding it in effective memory, and maintaining the commitment that grows out of the experience. We once had a vision of ourselves as dedicated, as ready to serve. We try not to lose that vision in the day-to-day tasks of ordinary life, but to shape a style of life that allows us to be true to the vision. We are faithful to these transitory but essential insights. One of our major tasks, then, is to remember who we are, which is to remember that we once were — and thus may again hope to be — in touch with what is most real. So much of our living as we are meant to live depends on our recollection. The pious person, Heschel says, "moves always under the unseen canopy of remembrance."[6]

72

When we remember who we are, we are remembering a relationship to what is most real. But since we find reality and value in and through our relationships in this world, we are also remembering all the people with whom we are connected. We remember those who have nourished, supported, and sustained us; we remember the places and the institutions where we have lived out our commitments; we remember the work that has been given us to do.

Sometimes we rely on others to remind us of who we have been and who we hope to be once again. Over the course of a life, we have sometimes had to put aside our earlier dreams. We are grateful to friends of long standing who remember our youth and young ideals and who see our present lifestyle as a detour. These friends help us find our way back.

In many respects, day-to-day life can be like the wilderness, with unsheltered areas, raw weathering, and blowing sands. In the desert there are structures called *Zeugen*, or witnesses. They are pillars that stand as witnesses to what was once a high plateau or stratum of rock. The friends of our youth are Zeugen in the desert of our lives. They bear witness to our earlier ideals and to the values that led us to choose these friends as companions. If we have lost the desire to return to our deepest dream, we may find ourselves uncomfortable with these Zeugen. But if the dream still lives, we find in their living memory the support we need.

RITUALS OF RELATEDNESS

Life intensifies through our awareness of its interrelationships and our celebration of them. Awareness includes both a quality of attention and a mode of action. This combination results in what I have earlier termed rituals of relatedness. Too often religious rituals have focused primarily on our relationship to God, with God understood as radically other. But when God is found in and through creation, we need to expand our sense of religious rituals to include our many relationships.

The function of ritual is to make us aware, to focus our attention, to remind us, to reconnect us to those who have gone before us and to those who are yet to come. As we think about ritual we become aware that we have created ritual all our lives. We haven't always given our own practices the authority and seriousness they deserve, but we do have our own ritual voice and we should recognize and celebrate it.

We use ritual acts as mnemonic devices for remembering who we are. We can have rituals of relatedness to family, to friends, to our work, or to our home. Our rituals can serve as explicit reminders of times when we, as a people or as individuals, stood in the presence of the holy. They exist precisely in the tension between habit and attention. By habit we shape ourselves as faithful people; through attention we aim for the creative and the spontaneous.

Ritual requires discipline and recurrence. We all have patterns of living that we repeat and that, through repetition, nourish us. But the repetition ceases to be nourishing and becomes deadening instead when it does not come out of our own inner nature but is alien and enforced from without. It is then no longer a means of remembering who we are, but one of forcing ourselves to become the person someone else thinks we should be. The ritual is nourishing only when it is grounded in our truest sense of our self. Our ritual, our practice, is a way of remembering who we are and a way of etching ever deeper the pattern we have discovered.

ECCLESIASTES VS. THE SONG OF SONGS

We cannot overestimate the centrality of memory to our lives. Memory can transform time, and memory is strengthened and renewed through rituals of relatedness. The Book of Ecclesiastes, traditionally attributed to Solomon, presents us with a severe test of our efforts against deadness. For Ecclesiastes, even memory seems an inadequate tool with which to overcome the opponent, time. Ecclesiastes also presents us with a powerful portrayal of the problem of time. Both models of time, cyclical and linear, that were current in biblical culture, are treated but Ecclesiastes focuses on the negative aspects of each. The view of time as cyclical (every year spring ripens into summer, then gives way to fall and winter, and then inevitably returns) is seen to rule out any notion of progress and to fail to offer renewal. A view of time as linear (time follows a unidirectional path from a beginning in time to an inevitable end of days) is seen to demonstrate our inevitable progress toward death, without concomitant progress in maturity and wisdom. Ecclesiastes exhibits weariness of the most acute form. Consistent with its misrepresentation of time is its misrepresentation of love and, more fundamentally, of God and of our relationship to God. The author's weariness can be answered simply by pointing out the bad arguments in the book. But a more striking answer to Ecclesiastes lies in another text attributed to Solomon, the Song of Songs.

Time in the Song of Songs is neither cyclical nor linear, because it is regarded as *duration*, not as perspective. Perspective is our view of time: how past is related to present and future. Duration is our experience of time: how time feels. When we emphasize the experience of time, the problems arising from a spatial model of time disappear. The problem of death is countered by the force of love — love is fiercer than death. In Ecclesiastes God is gingerly approached with ritual correctness. In the Song of Songs God is as present as the very air we breathe — so present and so lacking in otherness that God is not addressed or even mentioned in the entire text.

Let us explore these points more fully to see if the Bible offers a way beyond weariness. The opening line of Ecclesiastes declares the problem:

> Vanity of vanities, says Koheleth, vanity of vanities, all is vanity. What profit has a man of all his toil beneath the sun? One generation goes and another comes, but the earth is forever unchanged. (Eccles. 1:2–4)

The problem begins with the position that life is not intrinsically valuable. Work is a burden unless it leads to some profit beyond itself. Much of the text explores these possible profits: fame, wealth, status, sexual partners, food, drink, etc. The text details the emptiness of each of these rewards. We begin to reflect on time as perspective when our experience of time as duration is unsatisfactory. This is a very helpful way of dealing with discomfort that must be endured for a limited amount of time. It is, however, not a useful way of viewing life as a whole. Ecclesiastes seems to agree: "There is no greater good for man than eating and drinking and giving himself joy in his labour." (Eccles. 2:24)

Joy of Process

But "joy" remains an undefined term. Joy can be dismissed too easily as pleasure or happiness. If it is, it will not carry the weight essential for responding to Ecclesiastes' challenge. Joy, according to Spinoza, is the move-

ment from a lesser to a greater perfection. This definition assumes that we are something that is in process and
that the process can be expansive (as it is in the Song
of Songs) or constricting (as it is in Jonah). We are trying to be more deeply connected to all that surrounds
us. This connection is through awareness, through ap-
preciation, and through service. In other words, there
is something we are trying to be *and* trying to do. Perhaps we become that something *through* what we do.
Perhaps a way of laboring can expand us — labor in terms
not only of employment but of a more extensive sense
of task. We have felt, from time to time, that something
is being asked of us, that we are called upon to do something. The idea that there is something we are called
upon to do implies that our lives are not the sole measure of the *value* of our lives. We are part of something
larger than our own lives and efforts. Although the meaning of our lives may not be clear, we know that they do
have meaning.

6

Love

Ecclesiastes gives us a clear formulation of the problem. The Song of Songs responds to the weariness of time in terms of love. Love is undefined but because it is so central, we need a definition that allows us to see how it can overcome Ecclesiastes' weariness. Love, according to Spinoza, is joy (which he defines as passage from a lesser to a greater perfection) with the accompanying idea of an external cause.[1] Implicit in this definition is the idea that there can be growth and transformation and that there exists some standard or notion of perfection. The definition also directs our awareness to what is around us. Something or someone outside of ourselves draws us out and expands us. As we continue perfecting our self for what we are called upon to do in this world, we discover that we are not alone. There have always been people who have helped others become who they were meant to be. But the problem in Ecclesiastes is not solely one of moving toward perfection. It is also that all life, human or animal, perfect or imperfect, must end in death. Between the first and ninth chapters, concern in the book shifts from the exhaustion brought on by the contemplation of cyclical time—

The sun rises and the sun sets, breathlessly rushing towards the place where it is to rise again. (Eccles. 1:5)

79

— to the fear of death:

> This is the root of the evil in all that happens under the sun — that one fate comes to all. Therefore men's minds are filled with evil and there is madness in their hearts while they live, for they know that afterwards — they are off to the dead! (Eccles. 9:3)

How can love take us beyond the dread of death? It is important that we think about the power of love with Spinoza's definition in mind. Something that turns us back in on ourselves may be powerful, but by Spinoza's definition would not be love. Love should enlarge our world and our concern for it. People who are "so in love" that they are indifferent to the world and to the cares of others are, by this test, not in love at all.

LOVE AND TIME

We have discussed love in terms of the spatial notion of expanding boundaries. We should also explore it using the temporal notion of present (duration) or future (perspective). Love appears to be outside the domain and dominion of time. In this regard, love differs from other emotions, which do have a temporal reference. Psychoanalyst Peter Hartocollis, building on the earlier work of Karl Abraham, addresses this issue:

> As Abraham observed, "anxiety and depression are related to each other in the same way as are fear and grief. We fear a coming evil; we grieve over one that has occurred." What relates these affects to each other is a temporal frame of reference. Anxiety, like fear, refers to a "coming evil"; depression, like grief, to "one that has occurred." Psychological or experiential time is a qualitative determinant of affects. [2]

The affects which Hartocollis analyzes in terms of time include boredom and depersonalization, guilt, fatigue, anger, euphoria, and hope. In contrast to these affects, he notes "that a pleasurable affect without reference to time, future or past, may be identified . . . as joy."[3]

Three centuries earlier, Spinoza drew up a similar catalogue of the emotions and observed their temporal component. The emotions he shows as having this temporal aspect are hope, fear, confidence, despair, gladness, remorse, repentance, self-exaltation, shame, and regret. He sought to experience everything under the aspect of eternity — that is, outside the domain of time (eternity being not the time that comes after time, but something altogether outside the realm of time). Spinoza found that what is outside the domain of time is the intellectual love of God. The same idea that Spinoza expressed in rationalist terms in his *Ethics* appears in the deeply moving poetry of the Song of Songs. Though formulated differently, both books provide the same answer to the problems of weariness, of boredom with self, and of time weighing heavily upon us. The answer lies in open awareness, noncalculative thinking, and being in the present, which is the only point where we can experience the sacredness of presence.

The experience of the present (time as duration) is part of the experience of love. We cannot know whether one causes the other, but we must recognize that a quality of attention is related to love. As we have seen repeatedly, the way we think and feel about this world radically transforms our way of being and acting.

The different sorts of attention entailed by time as perspective and time as duration are described by Joanna Field.[4] One sort is our everyday, automatic kind of attention. We look at things in order not to bump into them or in order to use them. We are "questing beasts"

81

and all the things that surround us become objects of our quest. The world is filled with objects, and we are alone with our own subjectivity. Another mode of attention occurs when we are still, cease our questing, and see the world as it truly is and not merely as it is for us. It is then that its wonder can rise up and amaze us.

The experience described by Field that allows us to drop our weariness and self-boredom is clearly the same one described in the Song of Songs as being full of the beauty and wonder of the natural world. How can we experience this beauty? Field's response is in terms of a form of consciousness or awareness she calls "wide attention." Spinoza describes this same form of consciousness as "the perception arising when a thing is perceived solely through its essence."[5] Things are perceived for what they are and not for what they are to us. Implicit in this form of consciousness is a profound statement of value, that we should hold things as valuable regardless of whether or not they contribute. Spinoza's discussion of this way of perception is especially significant because it represents his solution to a problem that is also found in Ecclesiastes. Like Ecclesiastes, he formulates the problem in terms of vanity:

> After experience had taught me that all the usual surroundings of social life are vain and futile . . . I finally resolved to inquire whether there might be some real good having power to communicate itself, which would affect the mind singly, to the exclusion of all else.[6]

Field asks for wider attention; Spinoza asks us to perceive things as they are in themselves and not as they are for us. Buber asks us to enter into an I-Thou relationship with things. When we know a thing as *It*, we know it as an object for our own subjectivity. When we know a thing as *Thou*, we know from within the being's

own subjectivity, or as if from behind its own eyeballs.[7]
We change our perspective by de-centering ourselves, and
entering a world of other subjects. To do that is to enter
a world with many competing centers of meaning and
value and to recognize the diversity and mystery implicit
in such a world. Dunne asks us to "pass over."[8] Passing
over is a shifting of standpoint. It is the experience of
entering sympathetically into the life and way of life of
another. Clearly Dunne is pointing the way to a quality
of awareness and attention, but implicit in that way are
commitment and action. Whether we call it wide attention, a way of perceiving, I-Thou relation, or passing
over, we are referring to a form of love that can respond
to the weariness expressed in Ecclesiastes.

FRIENDSHIP

Love is not restricted to the relationship between lovers. Our closest friends are co-creators of *our* world. We
create our relationship and we create a shared view of
our world. Entering into such a relationship is analogous
to the biblical notion of making a covenant. The biblical covenant is not like a contemporary contract. The
model of God's covenant with humanity is reflected in
the marriage vow. Biblical characters married first and
then came to love — because of shared experiences, ob-
stacles overcome together, shared affection for the children, etc. So the relationship we have with our friends
is one of commitment which engenders love. The more
we share and the more we put into the relationship, the
more deeply it nourishes us.

In our discussion of space, we saw how friendship helps
transcend the boundaries between people. In our discussion of time, we saw how friendship is related to mem-

ory and to trust in the future. Friendship gives us our world and also enlarges and challenges our sense of the world. Friendship is also something we can rely on. In that regard, seasons can be relied on, but does that make them friends? If we lived in conformity with nature then the seasons, even the harsh ones, would be our friends. When we understand the role played by the seasons, we find that even the so-called harsh ones have meaning. The same is true of the seasons of our lives. Whatever we understand and can rely on can be our friend. In principle, then, we can have friendship with old age, sickness, even death. Friendship is expressed in our rituals of relatedness that connect and reconnect us to our world. Friendship supports and sustains our world, but more than that, it helps create it.

Uses in Knowing

If we explore the fundamental areas of philosophy and try to locate where friendship ought to be discussed, we would probably choose ethics. Friendship is central to how we ought to live, though its importance is not restricted to ethical issues. It is also a central notion in epistemology (how we know) and metaphysics (the study of being). If we are to grasp the meaning of "understanding," we must examine friendship, which we have recognized to be an essential part of reality. The dyadic love portrayed in the Song of Songs and the wider love of friendship are essential to knowing and being.

The role of friendship in coming to understanding is expressed in Dunne's description of a festival night:

> It all seemed an image somehow of life's journey walking together in the dark, carrying our candles, and coming at

last into a place of light. . . . And yet life was not all darkness. There was the light of the candles we were carrying and there was the sharing of the light with one another as we relit one another's candles every time they were blown out in the wind. That is the essence of a way, that there be some mode of gaining life and some mode of sharing it with one another.[9]

We need to share light. We carry light within us; on occasion we give of the light and on occasion we receive light from others as our own fades. Sometimes a person who gives us light is someone to whom we had given light ourselves. At such times we may be amazed to have our own insight returned to us, applied now to our own situation. More often the receiving comes from one source and the giving goes to another. We don't always know to whom we have given, and some of the most precious light comes anonymously. Our light is not constant, but in sharing we endure.

This imperfect system of transmitting knowledge is not the only limitation in our seeking to know. We cannot know reality unless we know what we bring to it. We cannot know the color of a piece of cloth unless we know the color of the glass through which we perceive it. What do we bring to our perceptions?

I am blind because I cannot see my own face, but if my face is illumined I can comfort another person who can see it. So too another can comfort me.[10]

We need one another to mirror each other and to illuminate ourselves and each other.

So friendship is a way of knowing: it helps the flickering light endure through the sharing of light. It also helps us recognize what we bring to the knowing situation. Just as students need the guidance of their teachers,

teachers learn from the responses of their students. Indeed, students and teachers "enter into a community of learning for the sake of helping each other to attain self-realization, which in the Confucian sense is predicated upon the cultivation of human relations."[11]

Plato regards friendship as central to philosophy and treats it in an illuminating manner. His discussion of friendship is explicit in the dialogue *Lysis* but his views on friendship come through more clearly in his use of the dialogue method. Plato approaches all the questions in philosophy through dialogue, through which insight is given and received. He lets friendship function as an epistemological method — we come to know through human interaction. Plato's world view, his metaphysics, is discovered less in the explicit content of the dialogues than in his commitment to the dialogic process. His insistence that philosophy take place in direct discourse must bear on his understanding of the nature of reality. We perceive the world filtered through what we bring to the knowing process, so our perception can be distorted. But if the knowing process occurs within the framework of ongoing dialogue, we can learn to recognize what we bring to our perceptions and together correct and extend our insights.

CREATIVE POWER

Human friendship, as Martin Marty claims, "images the Way Things Are."[12] If we accept his view, then our experiences of friendship exhibit the structure of reality much as a fern segment exhibits the structure of the whole frond. It means that the joys we have in friendship are part of the nature of reality, as are the disappointments. The otherness that challenges and enlivens us individu-

ally challenges and enlivens reality as a whole. Marty
writes further:

> You will cherish friends most if you think of your relation
> to them as an act of creation and an act of freedom. Com-
> pare friendship to the creation of the universe.[13]

The creation of *the* universe is hard to think about. But
the creation of *our* universe is more to the point. Our
universe, as we have been realizing through the course
of examining the categories of space and time, lies in
the interaction of our subjectivity with the objective
physical world. Our world is neither solely "out there"
nor solely "in our mind" but is the result of the interaction between the two. Friendship perfectly images this
notion of *our* world. Our friends exist, with their particular qualities, before we come into their lives. We also
exist, with our own qualities. Now what makes other people our friends is not simply a result of our both having
certain qualities, but of our valuation of their qualities,
their valuation of ours, and our mutual creation of a relationship. *Together* we create something that takes on a
life of its own, our friendship. Friends become dear not
only for their intrinsic value but because of what we in-
vest in them. The amount of life, energy, and time we
pour into the relationship determines the relationship's
value.

We know a lot about friendship: what sustains it, what
threatens it, how it can electrify us, how it can grow cold.
Such knowledge teaches us much about our world: what
sustains it, what threatens it, how it enlivens us, and how,
without our conscious effort, it can grow cold. The fate
of our world is not left in the hands of some distant po-
tentate; it is something in which we are actively engaged.
To sustain the world, then, is to have a commitment to
it in friendship.

Love

THE THIRTY-SIX SECRET SAINTS

In Genesis we find the story of the destruction of the cities of Sodom and Gomorrah. Abraham pleads for the cities and God agrees that if ten righteous inhabitants can be discovered, the cities will be spared for their sake. If the cities are spared for the sake of ten, for how many does God spare the world? The rabbis decided that thirty-six righteous people keep God from destroying the world.

Jewish lore has produced story upon story about one or another person who is said to be one of the *lamed-vovniks*, the thirty-six secret saints for whose sake God sustains the world. They are said to emerge in the *shtetl* (village) just before the Sabbath, producing a fine Sabbath meal, a dowry for a bride, or one more way to ward off the Czar. But behind the folk tradition lies a profound insight. Whether or not *the* world is sustained by the thirty-six, *our* world is. It is sustained by many threads of connection — our family, our friends, our colleagues at work. We know when one of our thirty-six has died because we feel the emptiness and the sudden instability of our world.

LOVE AND MOURNING

When we realize that only a small number of people sustain our world, we recognize how central mourning must be. To love is to admit someone into our circle of secret saints and when one of them dies, our world is at risk.

> Tzu-yu said, "When mourning gives full expression to grief nothing more can be required."[14]

In mourning, our life-giving image of connection must

be replaced by Lifton's image of separation. But if we are to recognize the full dimensions of separation, we must first become aware of the intricacies of connection. A circle of the seasons gives us one connection.

If love can modify or transform our experience of time, then loss of loved ones must be experienced through our unaided perception of time. The lost ones are connected to time in terms of all the festivities and occasions of the year. They are connected to the past, and all of our memories are suddenly transformed because we look at the past with the present's awareness of loss. They are connected to the future, and as we face a problem or achieve a triumph we are aware that they will not be sharing it with us. They are connected to the present and to our loss of joy. We wonder if we will ever again experience time as we did when they were part of our world.

The connection is spatial as well. Certain places will always be associated with our lost ones: home, the place we met, the places we walked together, the places where they worked. Even people we knew together constitute connections. All of these connections must gradually be collected and recollected.

We might imagine that Lifton's image of disintegration foreshadows our falling apart. If our loved ones were at the center, wouldn't everything fall apart without them? But everything doesn't fall apart; things are shaky but the center can hold. Lifton's image of stasis is perhaps the most chilling. Stasis is surely the most difficult situation to get beyond. To exist and to endure are difficult enough, but we must also grow, move, and continue to evolve.

When we recognize that mourning lies deeper than time and space, we recognize that it must be explored through the most fundamental category of the mind, love. If it is deeper than time and space, then it is free from time and space. Such freedom (like all freedoms) can be either positive or negative in its implications. A wound of fifty years ago can be as fresh and painful as a current loss. But priority of love also means that separation can be understood and reconceived in a fresh way. Separation does not imply distance in space or distance in time. Rather, separation implies distance in memory, commitment, awareness, and concern. Perhaps in our process of collecting all our many connections, we are recollecting and regathering what has been lost. How can it be, when the center of our life is lost, that we do not fall apart? We almost want to fall apart — doing so seems easier than going on.

There is a time, shortly before spring, when it is good to repot plants. Perhaps repotting is a way to hurry the seasons. We might choose a gray, unhurried day and examine each plant one by one to see what new shoots have started up, to wash the leaves, freshen the soil, and divide the plants that threaten to outgrow their pots. Before a plant is divided it is rich, luxuriant, and overflowing its pot. After division, each of two pots contains something weak, fragile, and greatly at risk.

When we are deeply connected to another person, shoots spring out to combine the two into a fuller entity. We may not even be aware of the shoots as we live our daily lives, until we are divided from our loved one. We are left weak, fragile, and not accustomed to standing on our own. But slowly our roots deepen, the stalk strengthens, and we can stand strong and independent once again.

To exist is an achievement. To endure is a splendid affirmation. But existence is not static, and slowly the motion and rhythm of life overcomes stasis.

Love

LEVELS OF MOURNING

> There are three ascending levels of how one mourns: With
> tears — that is the lowest. With silence — that is higher. And
> with a song — that is the highest.
>
> (Abraham Joshua Heschel)[15]

How are we to understand this? Tears are essential and
they are our first reaction to loss. But as genuine and
as necessary as they may be, they are nonreflective. Loss
is an experience and tears are a reaction to the experience but not a reflection on it. Tears can bring real comfort, but they cannot produce insight.

Silence points to a deeper encounter with loss. Speech
occurs within a symbol system, language, that we share
in common with others. Just as the lesser lights in Genesis — the sun, moon, and stars — allow us to bring our private experience of time into the common experience,
speech allows us to do the same with our private experience of loss. But it is not possible to deal with our deepest
feelings within the limitations of language. Silence allows
us to reflect on our loss and to recognize wonder before
what is and what is no longer.

But song?

> He lifted me out of the miry pit, the slimy clay, and set my
> feet on a rock, steadied my legs. He put a new song into
> my mouth, a hymn to our God. (Ps. 40:3–4)

The full experience of loss may well entail a descent
into the miry pit and the possibility of further and further descent as the clay slides and our legs no longer support us. Depression and despair can deepen. But the very
process of entering fully into our grief can help us overcome it. The process cannot be hurried nor can anyone
guide us through it. What emerges is not only the per-

sistence of life but the insistence. Life is urgent! Beyond reason, beyond justification, our legs are steadied. When we have mourned fully we emerge, without any rational explanations for why the loss occurred or how we overcame it. What we have instead is a new relationship to the beings and objects in our lives. This new experience is the new song in our mouths and signals the end of mourning.

Mourning as Illustrated in the Book of Jonah

Jonah was living his life, with his own plans and agendas, when suddenly there was an irruption. He interpreted it as a call, though one he did not want to answer. We are free to interpret the transformations in our lives which take us away from our own private dreams and aspirations. We tend to call such irruptions "tragedies." They might well be tragedies, but they could also be opportunities to discover what we can do with what has been given to us. Jonah's choice of flight in an attempt to escape the call resulted in an experience of profound loss. Until he was called to go to Nineveh, he had a sense of himself as a God-fearing person. The implications of his religious commitment were now being demonstrated, and he was rejecting them. To be God-fearing is to put one's life at the disposal of God. But Jonah chose not to do that, so he lost a major sense of himself. In grief for the life he once had (or the sense of himself he was once able to maintain), he cut himself off from all other life. He became indifferent to the tempest that raged around his ship and to the fate of its sailors. His consent to being tossed overboard is consistent with his grief. His experience of constriction (in the whale) is also consistent. When he first becomes aware of his loss, he calls out to God. In giving voice to his grief he takes a more active role in the mourning process. But he is far from finished. The episode of the gourd provides a further lesson in mourning. What is real, what we must cherish, is whatever will further God's way. The Book of Jonah begins with Jonah's being called away from his own aspirations to do the will of God. The book ends with Jonah's not having learned the lesson and once again focusing on *his* own interest, only to discover that all, all is God's. We learn to love and we learn to let go. Those we admit to our circle of secret saints sustain our world and in their demise they threaten it. But we bless those who pass into our lives and we bless them on their going forth, and we remember. The process of letting go is a very slow and painful one, but we go through the process because our world is at stake.

Friendship and love help us to know reality. They also constitute part of reality and their loss puts everything at risk. But the risk can be overcome within the biblical way of life. The biblical way of life is a way of understanding and a way of acting. At its heart is love, a term that holds for the relationship between lovers in the Song of Songs as well as it does for the relationship between friends. Love is not only a way of thinking but a way of acting. It is this love, as action, that can carry us beyond mourning to renewed joy. Love as action is illustrated in the precepts, "You shall love the Lord your God with all your heart and with all your soul and with all your might" (Deut. 6:5) and "Love your neighbor as yourself" (Lev. 19:18).

We are accustomed to think of these two statements as commandments and at the same time to believe that love is not the sort of thing that can be commanded. And yet we agree that these are the essential values taught in the Bible. How then are we to understand them and to shape our lives in terms of them?

LOVE AS ACTION

Love is a way of being and of doing, yet it seems to elude us. Perhaps that is so because love is an accompaniment to right action, not a substitute for it. In other words, love is an epiphenomenon, like happiness. According to Aristotle, we cannot go after happiness; rather, we go after a certain activity and discover in the process that we are happy. There can be no direct going after happiness, and the attempt is not only logically impossible but experientially self-defeating. In the same way, there can be no direct going after love. Love is the accompaniment to a wide variety of deeds, transforming each into something of transcendent worth.

> The Master said, "Is benevolence really far away? No sooner do I desire it than it is here." (Confucius)[16]

Love can be here at our desiring only if it is an action rather than a passion. Passion is what we suffer, that is, what is done *to* us, rather than what we do. We are accustomed to thinking of love as a passion. Accompanying this idea of love is the corresponding notion of *falling* in love, with all its implications of losing control, choice, stature, and dignity. But if love is something we do, something we choose to shape our lives around, rather than something that is done to us or befalls us, then we do not *fall* in love, we *grow* in love.

I do not mean to dismiss spontaneous moments of a felt experience of love. These momentary experiences serve to remind us of value and demand a response on our part. If they are simply passions, they come and go and are not the basis on which to build or shape a life, but they can serve a significant function. The experience of love is analogous to that of wonder: suddenly the ordinary is extraordinary. How can separate instances of wonder be linked to become a way of perceiving the world? This is Joanna Field's question in *A Life of One's Own* and Spinoza's question in *On the Improvement of the Understanding.* How do we culture individual insights into a form of consciousness? How do we go from love as a passion to love as an action?

Love as an action means being concerned with day-to-day life, with the common deeds, the little details, the apparent trivialities of daily concerns. In describing another era, Heschel writes:

> The predominant feature of the biblical pattern of life is unassuming, unheroic, inconspicuous piety, the sanctification of trifles, attentiveness to details.[17]

We must sustain love, and life; we must struggle for peace and meaning. We must sustain relationships, recommit ourselves day in and day out. Our commitment must be like our breathing: we breathe in or out at every moment and we accept the ongoingness and continuation of that process.

ACTIVE LOVE THROUGH THE TEN WORDS

One way that love grows is through living a life according to the Ten Commandments, as the passage in Exodus 20:1–14 is commonly called. The introductory sentence of the passage reads, "God spoke all these words [Hebrew: *devarim*]. . . . " When referring in Hebrew to the passage, Jews still use the expression *'aseret ha-dibrot,* which translates as "the ten words." Ten Words actually describes the passage much more accurately than Ten Commandments, and the distinction is significant. When we think of commandments, we think of rules, laws, and injunctions; we think of punishments, rewards, and standards to be measured against — all of which point to an external judge. Ten Words, on the other hand, is neutral and allows us to approach the passage without a prior mindset. According to the Masoretic tradition, the first of the Ten Words is, "I am the Lord your God who brought you out of the land of Egypt, the house of bondage." If we are looking for commandments, we are bewildered by this statement because it does not appear to command anything. In many traditions it is in fact joined to the next statement, "You shall have no other gods beside Me." But if we are not approaching the text as commandments, we can pause and try to understand what the text conveys. Focusing now on the text, we may wonder why the creator of heaven and earth neglects to mention these, choosing instead to be identified only as God who liberated the people from Egypt. The answer lies in the circumstances of the events at Mount Sinai. The Ten Words were addressed to those people who had just come out of Egypt a few weeks earlier. God says to them, in effect, I am the one you have met in your experience of liberation from bondage. As we read the text, we must insert the characterization that gives us a personal meaning to the title God: I am the one you met when your first child was born; I am the one who comforted you when you thought life could never again be meaningful; I am the one who made it possible for you to love. God is the God *met in experience.*

The second of the Ten Words follows inevitably from the first: "You shall have no other gods beside Me. You shall not make for yourself a sculptured image, or any likeness of what is in the heavens above, or on the earth below, or in the waters under the earth. . . . " Once we know that God is the God met in experience, we cannot be confused about who God is. The temptation to idolatry is the temptation to inauthenticity. If we take other people's experiences more seriously than our own, we become estranged from ourselves. God is urgent and imperative only if God is relevant to our own life, and that happens when God is discovered in and through our life.

The third of the Ten Words, again, follows directly from the previous ones: "You shall not swear falsely by the name of the Lord your God." Words can heal only if they are taken seriously. Language can liberate, bless, or transport us only if it is used with the care and reverence that precise attention allows. We must know what we mean when we say God — we mean to convey both an awareness of our own inability to conceptualize God and our gratitude for momentary experiences that affirm the reality of the wondrous.

"Remember the sabbath day and keep it holy." Too often we judge the value of something in terms of an end or goal. We forget that there is intrinsic value, that things are valuable before they contribute. Periodically our standard must be challenged. We are made to accept reality as it is, without our transforming it. On the sabbath we cannot transform reality by cooking, by building, by spending money, or by rearranging. Normally we are called upon to do work, but once a week we recall that even when we do nothing, the world sustains and supports us. This fourth word, too, follows from the previous ones. As increasingly we locate the meaning of God in our experiences, we begin to trust them more. We come to trust that this is a world in which we can, from time to time, find rest and thus restored, return to make our contribution.

"Honor your father and your mother. . . ." The fifth word is important not only for what it says but for what it does not say. It does not tell us to honor our good or honorable parents, it tells us to honor our parents. We are to honor them because we are to honor ourselves. We carry our parents within us. As we grow closer to becoming who we wish to be, we grow to respect the source of our lives, even if the source is imperfect. Blaming our parents marks an inability to get on with life. It also serves as an analogue to our blaming of God. Our lives may not be what we would wish them to be, but our task is to transform our lives, not to blame our source.

"You shall not murder." The sixth word follows from honoring our parents, the source of our life. The word grows out of an increasing awareness of how great is the gift of life. Rather than being commanded, we are being tempered by these words.

"You shall not commit adultery." As we become familiar with love through loving our parents and, by extension, loving other people's parents, we begin to see the flaw in adultery. We may once have thought that love depended on the object of love, so when love began to feel less electrifying, we searched for a new object to love. But now we begin to recognize that adultery is an expression of deadness, a reflection not on the former loved one but on the self. We cannot turn the clock back to a time of young love. Love depends on what we bring to love — our own commitment based on finding God in and through our experiences. When our love ceases to be fresh and vibrant, we must look to ourselves. Often our lack of delight is caused not by any objective change in our loved one, but by something that has deadened us to what is wonderful in the one we used to love.

"You shall not steal." Stealing is claiming for our own what is not ours. As we become increasingly aware of all that has been given to us and all that nourishes and sustains us, we recognize that God is the true owner of everything in the world. We steal not only when we take something that is claimed by someone else, but also when we use our talents (our gifts) for our own aggrandizement rather than for the contribution we are to make to our world. We should see no need to steal because we periodically experience that the world will sustain us. We should be learning that we need not clutch, grasp, control. As we grow in trust, stealing becomes foreign to us.

"You shall not bear false witness against your neighbor." Each of the Ten Words deepens our sense of personal value. Bearing false witness would be inauthentic. As we become increasingly valuable to ourselves, we find it less and less acceptable to compromise our sense of truth. It is in the truth of our being that we have found God and we dare not compromise that.

"You shall not covet. . . ." As we shape our lives from word to word, we find the shape of our dreams and desires changing. We do not have to grit our teeth to avoid desire. This last word simply describes what will follow if we live a life grounded in the experiential knowledge of God. We can understand love more deeply when we take The Ten Words as descriptive rather than prescriptive.

The way of loving is a way of doing, of being, of relating. Sometimes it is accompanied by feeling, sometimes the feeling eludes us, but always the commitment remains.

7

Life in Death

Behind, beneath, supporting all the other symbols and images is the one most fundamental of all, meaning. It is an affirmation that everything we do, experience, and suffer is part of a meaningful system; that we have a function, and that our contribution is essential. Within the biblical structure of the world this meaning is easy to affirm. From the opening lines of Genesis, which affirm the primacy of light and, by extension, consciousness, awareness, and sense, to the Ten Words of Exodus 20 which affirm that there are better and less good ways to live, we are taught that there is something we are supposed to be doing, learning, and being. In order to fulfil our charge we must stay conscious of our situation and aware of our choices.

When we experience deadness, one of the crucial things that is destroyed is our sense of self. The way in which we know ourselves largely determines how we experience our world and our relationship to it. If knowledge of ourselves is fundamentally material (for example, chemical, biological, or statistical), we have no way of relating what is most intimate to ourselves with the rest of our experience of the world. We can experience

101

ourselves as the product of the union of two cells, as the result of the love of two people, or as a creation of God. Each explanation incorporates the previous one but transforms our understanding of it. The latter explanation transforms our understanding of human love and sees it not as an end in itself but as part of a larger scheme of love. Theologian Robert Bilheimer points out:

> Because biblical people knew God, they knew the self. That was their principle of coherence. From the knowledge of God all else flowed.[1]

So if in understanding our origin we can go beyond the level of cells, and even the level of parents, our sense of ourselves is radically transformed. But we can have a deep understanding of self one day and forget who we are the next. This forgetting is very damaging, as Bilheimer also tells us:

> The human creature is of such a wondrous texture that if worship is given to anything less than God, the human texture falls apart.[2]

When we forget who we are, we are forgetting our essential relationships, because who we are is determined by them. Our relationships help define us and our most essential and enduring relationship is to God. Furthermore our relationship to God is not one among many, but the one that lifts up and encompasses the many. Our commitments, our loyalties, our faithful practices, our friendships are all part of our relationship to God. We approach God where we are, in the relationships in which we find ourselves, and in the work that is given to us to do. We cannot relate to God by shirking our other responsibilities.

The biblical notion of the call remains an imperative for us in our own times. We have all been called — into being (we did not create ourselves) and into meaning (our lives don't explain themselves). We are uniquely able to contribute something. We have sensed this imperative from time to time in our lives, but other sounds can drown out the essential call. The problem, in part, is that we don't understand the urgency of the call unless we know who is calling and thus, who we are.

In commenting on the story of the binding of Isaac, Jean Paul Sartre sees the essential question as being, "Am I Abraham?"[3] We must understand that our call is as serious as the call to Abraham. We must also understand that just as no one but Abraham is Abraham, no one but ourself is ourself. The glory of the call — and also its risk — is that it is always new, always uncharted, and can never be subsumed under a general category, "Abrahamic call." Each call is unique and addressed to only one person, and each person is called.

Call requires a caller, so in addition to the explicit content of the call we have the implicit message that God is present. By presence I mean the actual, felt experience of the presence of God. Terrien stresses that in Hebraic religion, the notion of presence has priority even over the notion of covenant:

> The reality of the presence of God stands at the center of biblical faith. This presence, however, is always elusive.[4]

Yet the very elusiveness of the presence is what brings us back, continually, to the notion of covenant. We can have experienced holiness, peace, wholeness, serenity, true joy, divinity; but in order to shape our lives around this experience, we need faith and faithfulness. Heschel teaches us that

> faith is the fruit of a seed planted in the depth of a lifetime. Faith is the fruit of hard, constant care and vigilance, of

insistence upon remaining true to a vision; not an act of inertia but an aspiration to maintain our responsiveness to [God] alive.[5]

I have defined faith as an experience held in memory that becomes a warrant for hope. Faithfulness is the practice built upon faith. Faithfulness is a life shaped by commitments, loyalties, and rituals of relatedness that help us hold in effective memory the experience of presence. We do not, and we cannot, always experience the presence, but we must be faithful to what we have known.

COVENANT

The experience comes and we must be open to it. We must hold it in memory and we must shape our life in accord with it through faithfulness. All of our individual acts of faithfulness then add up to a deeper covenant with being.

Time is one context within which we can experience the presence. We have holidays of awe and reverence and we have festival days of joy that encourage the experience. But we must also be open to experiencing the presence in our daily rounds and we must sustain the insight through the barren times. We can also experience the presence in the context of space. We may find the holy both in boundaries and in the breakdown of boundaries, but we must live out the implications of our discovery wherever we find ourselves to be.

Friendship may be the clearest context in which to think about covenant. Unlike a covenant, a contract spells out the obligations of both parties and their expected return. A covenant, in contrast, is a promise whose full implications we cannot understand at the time we make it, but whose maintenance will give shape to our lives. A covenant is a serious commitment that will carry us to an unknown but promised land. Becoming a parent is one experience we can have of entering a covenant. I cannot know what being a parent to *my* child will mean over a lifetime. I know only that for the rest of my life, my peace of mind is inextricably connected to the being and well-being of my child. Marriage is frequently a covenant. Some people no longer take seriously the phrase, "for better or for worse," but that is precisely what makes the relationship covenantal. I may enter a marriage and learn a month later that my spouse had just contracted a degenerative disease. To share that fate, because we are one flesh, is to enter into the wilderness of illness strengthened only by the force of covenant. Covenant brings with it both the experience of presence and the experience of absence. The covenant itself sustains us through the times of absence.

"The Parable of the Stranger" by philosopher Basil Mitchell gives eloquent expression to the meaning of covenant:

> In time of war in an occupied country, a member of the resistance meets one night a stranger who deeply impresses him. They spend that night together in conversation. The Stranger tells the partisan that he himself is on the side of the resistance — indeed that he is in command of it, and urges the partisan to have faith in him no matter what happens. The partisan is utterly convinced at that meeting of the Stranger's sincerity and constancy and undertakes to trust him.
>
> They never meet in conditions of intimacy again. But sometimes the Stranger is seen helping members of the resistance, and the partisan is grateful and says to his friends, "He is on our side."
>
> Sometimes he is seen in the uniform of the police hand-

ing over patriots to the occupying power. On these occasions his friends murmur against him: but the partisan still says, "He is on our side." He still believes that, in spite of appearances, the Stranger did not deceive him.[6]

Presence is always conditioned by absence because we cannot control the experience. When we lose faith, we sometimes look for it in the wrong way: "Israel has ignored his maker and built temples" (Hos. 8:14). People build temples in an attempt to locate God. But God is found everywhere, and nowhere. Every attempt to grasp the experience of presence, which is freely given and freely withheld, expresses our lack of faith and must fail. We may create holy days, but the patina of the holy can come to us on ordinary days just as easily (or with just as much difficulty).

Our friendships are shaped by our initial impressions of the "Stranger." We may go through arid times in a relationship when we do not experience the same closeness. But if we recall the initial meeting and persist in our commitment, we may be rewarded by a meeting on a deeper level, which reminds us that there really was a reason for our initial commitment. This deep meeting contrasts with our more usual meeting of people on the level of shared interests, common annoyances, humor, etc. It occurs on the level of our most essential self, in all our fears, hopes, and vulnerabilities. We meet in the solitude that is our own aloneness, but that is common to all human beings. Meeting there enables us to know each other not for who we appear to be, but for who we most truly are. We haven't been known in that way since infancy, when those who cared for us knew our needs before we could express them. Allowing ourselves to be fully understood is a gift to our friends and an even deeper gift to ourselves.

Life in Death

RITUALS AS LIFELINES

We shape our lives in terms of our experiences, using rituals of relatedness that form the contours of our lives. Jewish tradition holds that God renews the work of creation every day.[7] We, in the image of God, can do so too by the rituals of relatedness that constantly reconnect us to our basic commitments. When we strengthen the relatedness we experience joy; when we loosen the relatedness, we find the world growing stale. W. E. Orchard expresses this thought in a prayer:

> Perhaps we have grown careless in contact with common things, duty has lost its high solemnities, the altar fires have gone untended, Thy light within our minds has been distrusted or ignored. As we withdraw awhile from all without, may we find Thee anew within, until thought grows reverent again, all work is hallowed, and faith reconsecrates all common things as sacraments of love.[8]

Joanna Field locates repeated passages in her diaries that describe moments of joy. We can identify and recall similar moments. For me such a moment occurs when the cat is purring, the house is silent, and I enter my room, ready to give myself over to the book I want to read or the idea I want to pursue. Relatedness to our work can be found in moments when we recall that this work is what we were meant to do, or at least that it is a context in which we can do what seems most important. Our relationship to our home might be found in cleaning, not as an aesthetic project or to gain someone else's approval, but to shape our environment to our own standard. We might rearrange a pile of books and magazines. The books remain in essentially the same place, but the new arrangement says something about our perception of value, and the time invested in the project

107

is part of that value. We are related to our past, a relationship celebrated through retelling family stories, looking at photo albums, using objects that belonged to our grandparents, and passing down a song or a recipe. We are also related to our own bodies. Our relatedness to our own bodies can be expressed in rituals of cleanliness or exercise and in accepting our own flesh, with its limitations as well as its energies.

Our ties, strengthened by rituals of relatedness, are lifelines through which vitality flows. The word "religion" comes from the Latin root meaning to connect or to bind and indeed, our rituals of relatedness are profoundly religious practices. Although our religious commitment may sometimes take us out to the desert or lead us to a mountaintop, more often it requires faithfulness to the place, the context, and the community in which we have been set down. Walking the dog on a below-freezing morning in February is not usually thought of as a religious obligation. But we have established trust with the dog. Not to walk him would mean breaking down both the trust and the relationship with the dog. So without too much hesitation, we leave our warm bed to face the chill winds and keep our trust, with the dog and with the creation of which he is a part.

During the first three years in my new home, I enjoyed gardening. I put in bulbs, weeded assiduously, and even planted a tree. Then one day gardening became a chore. Keeping the house in order was difficult enough; did I have to be responsible for the land around the house as well? So I ceased gardening. One day months later I went out to the garden and discovered that it was alien. What had been an extension of our home had become something foreign, accusing, and certainly hostile. A piece of the world to which I had been connected had become disconnected. My relationship to the garden serves as a powerful analogy for what occurs when we allow ties to break.

Not everyone has a committed relationship with a garden and not everyone should. Choosing relatedness to a garden means defining ourselves in one way, just as choosing relatedness to music is defining ourselves in a different way. Relationships are investments of time and of energy. We uniquely choose our commitments and so uniquely shape our lives.

FAITHFULNESS TO TRADITION

We are faithful because of an initial experience of faith, an experience held in memory that becomes a warrant for hope and action. The experience might be one of connection, wonder, insight, awareness, or love. In the stress of day-to-day living, we could forget the wonder, dismiss the love, neglect the connection. But faithfulness holds in memory and practice the initial, essential insight and shapes a life around it. Earlier we discussed the sacred nature of our experiences, our commitments, and our relationships. Once we recognize that the holy resides in the ordinary, we acknowledge that we are our own sacramentalists. We must recognize that religion — the wonderful tapestry that interweaves, ties, and connects the fragments of our lives — is something we do together, as peers. We are human together, sharing the human condition. Together we attempt to create a vision of the world we can share.

Our created world is in part fresh and new and in part freshly discovered and recovered. We recognize the contribution of those who came before us. The importance of earlier contributions was already remarked on by Confucius: "I was not born with knowledge but, being fond of antiquity, I am quick to seek it."[9] In the Confucian tradition, knowledge encompasses recollection of and intense respect for history. The biblical tradition, as Heschel points out, similarly teaches us that the past is important and we should learn from it:

> This is the test of character — not whether a man follows the daily fashion, but whether the past is alive in his present. . . . Much of what the Bible demands can be comprised in one word: *Remember.* "Take heed to thyself, and keep thy soul diligently lest thou forget the things which thine eyes saw, and lest they depart from thy heart all the days of thy life; make them known unto thy children and thy children's children" (Deut. 4:9).[10]

The Bible remains an important starting point for us. We have in common what is human, and reflections on the human condition illuminate its pages. We do not come to the text passively; we use it to help us understand our own experiences and we use our experiences to help us understand the text. Our relationship to the text is a living one that grows with our own life. We relate to scriptural texts differently at different times in our lives. The passage we understood one way in early childhood takes on a new meaning when we read it as spouses or as parents. Different parts of the Bible speak to us in our differing circumstances. But the text continually gives us a place from which we gain perspective on our lives.

Our reverence for tradition begins with a recognition that we are rooted in what came before us. Our language, our customs, our initial way of looking at the world, were all gifts, a heritage from our ancestors. When we recognize that we are part of something larger than our own individual lives and efforts, we gain a deep respect for the contribution of all who came before us, and we aspire to make our own contribution. Our reverence should

include a healthy respect for the resiliency of the tradition. It *can* bear our scrutiny, our challenge, our modi-
fication, so we need not proceed with unquestioning awe.
Suppressing our questions would, in fact, convey a more
fundamental doubt than asking them. Having realized
that we carry the tradition within us, we can challenge
it as we challenge our own muscles to stretch a little further, to reach beyond where they reached yesterday, and
to become all they can become.

We also respect tradition because time and this world
are the location for meaning. We think about time rather
than passively accepting someone else's characterization
of it. Similarly we think about space and reflect on it
though finally we dismiss neither as illusory. Within the
raw materials of the time and space of this world we
can contribute to meaning and to the sense of the sacred. The sacred is not in opposition to the secular, it
is fashioned out of it. The Bible recounts the meanings,
the values, and the sense of the sacred that our forebears
fashioned out of the time and space allotted to them.
We find ourselves with some work that has been given
us to do, some people who have been given us to be
committed to, some place where we have been set down.
Our challenge is to make the work meaningful, to enter
into living, deeply nourishing relationships with the
people, and to make our space a holy land.

"I Believe, Help My Unbelief!" (Mark 9:24)

We believe imperfectly; we doubt along the edges. But
we know what to do with our doubt: we bring to it the
ontological argument or the *Kaddish* recited when we
are most vulnerable to doubt. Even our doubt can be
eased — doubt can be turned back on itself so that it af-

firms. Earlier we saw that Lifton's three images of death could be reversed into images of life. Space and time can also be images in which and through which we find life. If we use space as a way of locating and recognizing relationship, we open ourselves to all that space can allow us. Space can be understood in terms of our valuation or love as, for example, when we think of space as rootedness. Time can be understood similarly. Time can give aliveness, through memory and faith. Time is also central in process, movement, and change. And in time and through time, we can learn to let go. We keep discovering over and over the insight in Goethe's lines, "So, waiting, I have won from you the end: God's presence in each element."

Any thought or symbol pursued to its end returns to life. Space can divide us, but it can also open us up to our connectedness. Time can lead us to a vision of an end of days, but it can also lead us to a vision of renewal.

Freedom in Interpretation

One of our recurring insights is that we have tremendous freedom in how we choose to construe (and so help construct) our world. Not only are the three images of death also images of life, but time which gives rise to the negative notion of guilt can also give rise to the affirmative notion of integrity. We begin to sense what the mystics were hinting at by declaring that the void is the plenum, or emptiness is fullness.

The Bible illustrates our freedom in interpretation by offering two sets of opposing images to deal with death and continuity. The first image is the return to Eden, which itself arises in opposition to the expulsion from Eden. This image of a return, which underlies Chris-

tian doctrine, accepts the notion of a fall from an earlier, more perfect state and seeks to recover lost inno-
cence. Taking the text of Genesis 3 as its starting point,
it focuses on the tree of knowledge of good and evil and
the implications of our having eaten the fruit of that tree.
In order to undo the "fall," we must be very clear as to
the nature of the fruit and reject that fruit in our present life.

Three mutually compatible interpretations of the nature of the tree have seen offered. The first is that the
tree represents sexual knowledge, which is causally related to our entrance into generation and hence into degeneration. In other words, prior to eating the forbidden
fruit, Adam and Eve were asexual. A return to asexual-
ity is required for a return to Eden. The connection between sex and death is clear: without reproduction, we
could imagine an immortal pair. But if we choose immortality through our offspring, we must forego personal
immortality for their sake.

The second interpretation holds that the tree of knowledge represents worldly knowledge. For adherents of this
view, secular knowledge (science, history, literature, etc.)
is suspect.

Finally, the tree is said to represent moral knowledge.
This claim leads to the injunction in the Greek Scriptures to refrain from judgment.

The move out of Eden was the move into time. It was
the move into becoming—coming to be and passing
away, and thus into aging and degeneration. The world
of Eden is otherworldly. It is the world of the isolated
self, for although it is inhabited by both Adam and Eve,
they are thrust out of it when they come together. Each
by him/herself is immortal, but each represents a threat
to the other. When they come together, they abandon
personal immortality for immortality through offspring,

timelessness for an entry into time, isolation for union, and otherworldliness for a deep concern for this world.

The return to Eden tradition stands in opposition to the prophetic tradition of the Hebrew scriptures, which focuses on this world as seen in the light of transcendent values. The prophetic tradition focuses on this world as it is and, at the same time, as it can become. This vision of what the world can become is valuable only insofar as it is functional, because we are here to contribute to the transformation of the world. The image of the prophetic tradition is one of social concern and political action.

We have positioned meaning and value in the area between what is "out there" and what is within us and we have named this space "reality." We have seen that two people can be in the same room but in different realities. And we have seen that reality is or can be socially constructed — it is what we build together and then come to inhabit together. We did not, after all, invent language, painfully learning to move our tongues to form new sounds. We inherited it gratefully and we use it, for the most part, in socially determined ways. We did not invent the symbols which shape the way we comprehend the world. We inherited them from religious, philosophical, and psychological traditions. We use them also, for the most part, in socially determined ways. We slough off one that has fallen into disuse and reinterpret another, hoping in some small way to contribute to the reality we build together.

CONSTRUCTING REALITY TOGETHER

If we are to understand what it means to construct a reality together and to inhabit it together, we must

explore community and friendship. We have recognized
the importance of trusting our experiences, but we have
no guarantee that experience brings wisdom. For that
reason I have emphasized the importance of *insight* into
experience. Experience must be reflected on, thought
about, and the unconscious symbols that lead us to react as we do must be made conscious. We take the experience, which is private and unique, and subject it to
scrutiny, which is communal. Naming the experience
brings it to common ground. The reflectiveness and
thoughtfulness that we bring to understanding our experiences is our offering to a common reality.

We are born into a structure of many overlapping,
competing, and complex systems by virtue of our living
in this century, this country, this culture. But we do not
passively inhabit this reality: we begin to make small
changes that make it more suitable to our needs. My
house may have suffered from lack of care by its earlier
inhabitants and the pipes have burst. I cannot repair
them alone, but I can call in others to help me make
repairs. Together we search for solutions to the problem
and we try to determine if there is any structural damage. For a long time my concern had been on the level
of decorating. Now I am tearing out a wall, ripping up
a floor, exposing a rotting beam. I didn't realize I could
learn to use a hammer and a saw, nor had I been fully
conscious of how deeply committed I was to this dwelling. My companions and I are determined not to let it
rot out of neglect, blindness, or fear. I have not always
recognized how many of us are sheltered in the same
dwelling. Some oppose our use of hammer and saw—
they want to simply paper over the water-stained walls.
Others try to point out that the water continues to leak,
the rot continues to spread. Still others want to move
away or retreat to the back porch. But many are willing

to bring their talents, experience, and courage to make the structural changes that enable us to continue living in the house.

Our aim should not be simply to create cheerful people, or optimists who refuse to consider the possibility of structural damage. Our aim should be to create people who are awake, aware, and alive. We don't need to seek out despair, but we needn't fear it either, unless it is so deep that it fosters inertia. On the other hand, a determined cheerfulness in the face of grief must finally be self-defeating. The determined nature of such a stance betrays a deep-rooted pessimism. If we trust, then we trust that even our sorrow can find comfort and our despair will be healed. If we do not trust, we dare not let ourselves acknowledge these feelings.

We all live in the same dwelling, though we are not always conscious of our sharing one home. We go about our lives; we decorate; we break the leg off a chair and forget to repair it; we put up storm windows and someone expresses gratitude. Our lives are tied up with this house — this house we inherited but keep modifying. And although the house existed before we did, only our determination and hard work can insure that we, in time, will be able to pass it on. A house must not be allowed to wear out.

> These floors to be mellowed by our footsteps
> These walls to resound to our singing
> These lights to shine on our evenings together
> In joy, warmth, and comfort
> This house to make our own
> By living here fully
> In love and commitment.[11]

Pain that informs us is not overwhelming because we face it, not as an enemy that attacks, but as a messenger that instructs. Boredom that we examine and allow to teach us is not the affliction it would otherwise be. All those states of being and consciousness that can try us and wear us down take on a different aspect when we decide that they are meaningful. By believing that all we do and suffer here has meaning, we can transform suffering.

A meaning — but what meaning? It is remarkable how resilient we can be with just *a* meaning, but eventually we need some further characterization of *the* meaning. A deeper understanding of meaning requires increased awareness and a notion of value expanded to all people and even to all being. It requires us to see our lives as a process of tempering and refining. And it requires not just acceptance but active engagement.

We are not simply clay in the potter's hands. We become increasingly aware that a part of us is working alongside the potter shaping ourselves by our choices of images and symbols.

8

Universe As Home

I have tried throughout this book to show that every event in the life cycle presents us with a door, or an invitation to a deeper life. We often don't recognize a door unless we bang into it, and even an open door is easily overlooked. We tend to find a door only when we feel a barrier — pain, loss, illness, a creative block, depression or boredom — and then we discover that we can push against it. But a joyous event can be a door just as well, if only we ask ourselves the same probing questions when we experience joy, happiness, success, good health, love, and birth, that we ask when confronting pain.

I have focused on the door of deadness in life. My approach in exploring deadness has been neither to suppress nor to deny it, but rather to acknowledge it, claim the experience, and recognize the significance of our feelings of deadness.

Deadness, in a world that is alive and vibrant, suggests that something is *metaphysically* amiss in our relationship to reality. Somehow we have misconstrued and misconstructed our way of being in the world. Deadness, faced and explored, invites us to reconceive that way. It urges us to make conscious and explicit those symbols through which the world is mediated to us. Its acknowledgment can be an invitation to a spiritual adventure. Deadness repressed, denied, or ignored cannot serve these important functions. Only if we treat it as a symptom does deadness have valuable information for us.

EXPERIENCE AND SYMBOLS

Deadness is not something we think, it is something we experience. When we take the experience of deadness seriously, we also begin to validate all our other experiences. In and through our experiences we discover that something about our relationship with reality is wrong — that in some fundamental way our vision of reality is flawed. And in and through our experiences we will know when that flaw has been corrected. We will know that we have overcome deadness when we feel alive. So the authentic acceptance of our own experience is necessary for correcting our relationship to reality. It is a necessary condition but not a sufficient one.

Experience is a primary but not a final condition for religion. If religion is insight into experience, we cannot do without experience, but neither can we rest there. As we examine our own experiences, we become aware that our experiences are mediated to us by symbols. Symbols are a complex of sensations, images, and concepts, formed in pre-linguistic childhood and transformed as we grow into maturity. What is initially a physiological process becomes, over time, a psychological and philosophical process. This progression from physiological to philosophical symbols is the progression from biology to freedom. As we explore our own experiences and become conscious of our use of symbols, we come to recognize that "without our own contribution we see nothing."[1] And so in the domain of symbols we discover and begin to explore an area of freedom.

Earlier we examined three symbols of death. We saw that the three symbols — separation, disintegration, and stasis — are potent but ambiguous: they can be opened up to serve as symbols of life. We examined separation and with it the contrary notion of connection. It is important for us to recognize that we are all connected to everything. The task of religion is to make us aware and conscious of these connections and to strengthen and deepen them.

As we deepen our understanding of our interconnectedness, we become aware that our notion of the individual is incomplete. The individual is not in opposition to society. We are socially constructed and we represent individual configurations of what has been socially given. We are formed out of our family, our friends, our society, our loved ones. We carry within us those who have helped to form, nourish, and sustain us, and we transform these contributions. Connectedness is significant and life-giving, but separation does not always entail death.

Separation has a creative potential, as demonstrated by the incidents of creation through separation in the opening chapter of Genesis (light from darkness, heaven from earth, sea from dry land) and by the human experience of separation from the womb, which is essential to further growth. Separation entails new space, but we are free to view this new space as either threat or challenge.

Deadness also forces us to think about disintegration. We examine our lives and attempt to discover what holds them together. Clearly we value a sense of integrity, of wholeness, but it is somehow possible to disintegrate and re-form around a new center. We have lived through times of disintegration and re-formation. Exploring disintegration leads us to speculate on what holds us together while this process is going on.

121

Finally we looked at stasis and its life-affirming opposite, motion. We recognized the life-giving process of
motion, but saw that stasis could be life-affirming as well.
Stasis can be understood as a deep stillness that supports
life rather than opposes it. So we see that the so-called
symbols of death need be no less life-affirming than any
other symbols, when they are deliberately and consciously explored.

SPACE AND TIME

The categories that are most difficult to examine, because we generally don't think of them as symbols at all,
are the symbols of space and time. That space is not a
"given" but is open to contradictory interpretation is an
important and potentially liberating insight. It allows
us to rethink and re-view the ways in which we normally
use the concept of space. One crucial notion that can
be transformed by our thinking about space is that of
boundaries between people. As we think about the ways
we use space, we realize that the boundaries between
people are not really absolute. They seem more formid-
able in the presence of fear and seem permeable in the
presence of love. Our exploration of the symbol "space"
allowed us to examine seriously the unthought-through
notion of otherness, which appears to be directly related
to fear. Once we recognize the role of fear in the estab-
lishment of otherness, we discover that death — often seen
as the absolute other — is not other at all but an aspect
of our own life that we carry within us. In claiming our
own death, we go beyond the fear to an acceptance of
the human condition that allows us to view with compassion all that lives and ages.

Time too is a symbol, in just the same way that space

has been shown to be. Time has two very different aspects. One focuses on the relationship of past, present, and future. In its developed form it gives rise to a view of individuality, with its companion notions of uniqueness and tempering through experience. It is essentially "spatial" in its formulation and suggests a particular viewpoint or way of ordering experience. Both linear time and cyclical time are examples of time as perspective. Another aspect of time, duration, is experiential and is focused on the present. It carries with it a mode of consciousness that allows us to go beyond deadness and the sense of vanity illustrated in Ecclesiastes to the sense of love and joy that pervades the Song of Songs. These biblical texts suggest that love and joy are available to us only in the present and only when we are fully open to the present, not ordering our experiences in terms of perspective.

The experience of time and the promise of an ongoingness of time always brings us back to a notion of faithfulness — faithfulness to our daily rounds, to our ordinary concerns, to our practices in which we live out our commitments. As we explore the relationship of time to faith, we realize that we can find the holy within the warp and woof of ordinary life. Our daily commitments and practices, the little events that make up the flavor of our lives, include not just arduous battles and shattering insights but also small tasks to do, children to care for, long winters and bouts with the flu to overcome.

In many different ways we are made aware that we are bodied people living in a world where daily physical concerns are an integral part of our lives. The experiences of daily life, the rhythm of meals and caring — all these are real and important. At times we may long to throw off the routine, but our disembodied desires can be a trap. God is found in and through our everyday, ordinary, trivial, mundane concerns. Our ordinary roles educate us.

LOVE

There is a symbol that is prior even to space and time. That symbol is love. Love is the essential substance of meaning and value; it helps create and support our world and because it does, our world is threatened when those we love die. Because of the central role played by love and by our loved ones in creating our world, learning how to mourn their loss is vital to our well-being. If we have not learned how to mourn fully, we are incapable of becoming fully alive. When someone we love dies, our first reaction is to fall into a numbness not unlike the sensation we feel when a limb "falls asleep." We must not remain in this state of numbness. We must restart the flow of blood through the sleeping limb. Dunne describes the process: "There is pain at first, but when sensation has returned fully there is a sense of well-being."[2] Our fear of mourning reflects our fear of this pain. We would prefer to forget but if we did, we would lose what was really nourishing about the love — then the person would be really dead to us. We would also lose that part of our self that was connected to the one we lost. Pain is endurable; we can grow through pain, although we'd prefer to grow in some other way. If we continue to think about what we have lost, reexamine, re-vision, and rethink it, its living aspect can be released to nourish our being once again.

Our love of others is not only essential for our discovery of meaning and value, it is also essential for our knowing. We are limited by our own perspective. Left to ourselves we could not get out of the limited angle of vision we bring to reality. But we can interact with other people and thereby learn that we are perceiving the world through our particular use of symbols. One use of our love of others, then, is negative — to remind us that we do *not* know, to bring us to the knowledge of ignorance. But while we begin by negation, we move on to affirmation. If what we thought was reality was merely our perception of reality, we still need to find an alternative vision. We can find one through our relationship to others as well. By being open to their vision, we can "passover" to it and so enlarge and enhance our own. Love becomes a way of recognizing our own limitations and going beyond them through compassion, seeing the world through another's perspective. But love is also a way of knowing, in that whole areas of reality are shut off to us except through love. We cannot, through an objective approach, know another being in its subjectivity. We can treat subjects as objects; but to know another's subjectivity, to understand from within, requires love.

MEANING

Finally, we have seen that the symbol beneath, behind, and supporting all the others, is that of meaning. To think about meaning is to explore not only which symbols we use, but what responsibility we have in their employment. We can use symbols automatically and unthinkingly; or, we can consciously and deliberately examine, adopt, and modify the symbols to create a world view that strengthens our relationship to reality. If boredom is a valuable symptom informing us that we have misconstrued or misconstructed reality, then we must examine carefully the symbols we employ. We share responsibility for a creative vision broad enough to encompass all humanity.

By affirming the reality of meaning, we affirm that

all we do in life can be shaped around our fundamental commitments. Loyalty to our friends takes on cosmological significance when we see it as part of the larger context of covenant. Faithfulness to our practice, awareness of and concern for all that surrounds us are part and parcel of our commitment to meaning.

The importance and ultimate significance of our faithfulness becomes even clearer as we try to understand what obstructs our joy. If we can sense the freedom that lies in our interpretation of symbols, why do we not face separation, disintegration, and stasis, with hope? What is it that makes time weigh heavily upon us or leads us to see it as pointing inevitably to death? What leads us to erect boundaries between ourselves and others and to close ourselves off from love? The barrier that closes us off from vitality, energy, and zest for life is fear. Fear directly opposes meaning and deadens us to our world.

Fear

We can see how fear closes us off if we examine our response to separation. In early adulthood, separation is an occasion for joy and adventure; at other times, it is an occasion for retreat. We see the results of fear in our response to disintegration and reintegration around a new center. Sometimes in our lives, disintegration calls us out of ourselves and we respond with some trepidation, perhaps, but with basic optimism. At other times, however, it causes us to hold on to the center even if doing so is inauthentic or damaging. Fear causes us to move in frantic ways when stillness may be what is called for.

The power of fear transforms our notion of space. Instead of envisioning space as "opening out," we tend to seek the enclosing space, fearing the loneliness of empty space. We tend to think of our personal space, our place, as fixed and we find change threatening. Perhaps nowhere is the obstructiveness of fear more obvious than in our relationship to otherness. Otherness and the resulting diversity can be enriching and exhilarating. In a fearful context, however, we do not allow ourselves to be open to the other, but we become defensive and closed off.

Fear is also a major component in our deadening interpretation of time. Fear prevents us from being in the present; it makes us leap ahead in anxiety and look back in regret. It closes us off to the possibility of renewal.

Fear prevents us from loving. It leads us to weigh the benefits and risks of relationship rather than opening us up to greater connectedness. We fear that our love may not be reciprocated or that even if it is, the one we love may be lost to us through death. We fear remembering those we lost because we think the memory will recall the pain.

Fear is the single greatest threat to meaning because meaning requires trust in a larger pattern. Meaning requires that we let go of our narrow perspective and look beyond our self to some greater call. But the fearful person is afraid to leave the security and familiarity of the self, however limited, for the vast expanses of an unknown. All three patriarchs, Abraham, Isaac, and Jacob, were called out of themselves and out of the context in which and through which they had come to form an identity, in order to find meaning in some larger scheme of things. The call did not end with the patriarchs — we are still being called to make the choice against fear.

OUR RESPONSE

The tools we need to overcome fear, and so to come fully alive, are ones with which we are already familiar. The first is faith. Faith is built up out of experiences that support it and that are held in memory. We already have a warrant for faith; we must become conscious of it and hold it in memory. Our other tool is faithfulness. We need habits of practice and perception that will support us through times when it seems that "the Stranger" is not on our side. In times of illness, loss, and pain, we can be sustained by a practice born out of an earlier time of faith. The faithfulness will carry us over these times. The practice, our rituals of relatedness, will sharpen our awareness of our interconnectedness, sustain the connection, and remind us of our being connected when it feels as though all our supports have been knocked out from under us. Fear may come but fear need not abide. We choose against fear: we choose life.

Our faith and our faithfulness constitute an important aspect of our religion. But the world is alive too, and as such transforms us as in turn we transform the world. The symbols serve as the way we come to understand and affirm meaning. We make a commitment to a symbol and let it shape us as in turn we shape it.

Together we are creating a place in which we can live. In creating this place we must remember that a house can become merely a material object, a possession, an interchangeable abode, unless memory, hope, and love transform it into a home. What is true for the house is true for the universe. The universe can be a welcoming home to us through our sensitivity to the symbols of time, space, love, and meaning.

Notes

1. DEADNESS IN LIFE

1. St. Diadochos of Photiki, in *The Philokalia: The Complete Text, Compiled by St. Nikodimos of the Holy Mountain and St. Makarios of Corinth*, trans. and ed. G. E. H. Palmer, P. Sherrard, and K. Ware (London: Faber and Faber, 1979–), vol. I, p. 270, no. 58.
2. Evagrios the Solitary, in *Philokalia* I, p. 53, no. 1.
3. Ibid., p. 48, no. 16.
4. Baruch Spinoza, *Ethics, preceded by On the Improvement of the Understanding*, ed. James Gutmann (New York: Hafner, 1955). The argument is developed in part V, propositions XX through XXXVI (pp. 265–275).
5. Elena Malits, *The Solitary Explorer: Thomas Merton's Transforming Journey* (San Francisco: Harper and Row, 1980), p. 70.
6. Abraham Joshua Heschel, *Quest for God: A Journey into Prayer and Symbolism* (New York: Crossroad Publishers, 1982), p. 29.
7. St. Thalassios, in *Philokalia* II, p. 322, no. 51.
8. St. Anselm, *Proslogion*, trans. M. J. Charlesworth (Notre Dame, Ind.: University of Notre Dame Press, 1979), chap. 1, p. 111.
9. *Proslogion*, chap. 2, p. 117:

Well, then, Lord . . . we believe that You are something than which nothing greater can be thought. Or can it be that a thing of such a nature does not exist, since "the Fool has said in his heart, there is no God"? But surely, when this same Fool hears what I am speaking about, namely, "something-than-which-nothing-greater-can-be-thought," he understands what he hears, and what he understands is in his mind, even if he does not understand that it actually exists. For it is one thing for an object to exist in the mind, and another thing to understand that an object actually exists. . . . Even the Fool, then, is forced to agree that something-than-which-nothing-greater-can-be-thought exists in the mind, since he understands this when he hears it, and whatever is understood is in the mind. And surely that-than-which-a-greater-cannot-be-thought cannot exist in the mind alone. For if it exists solely in the mind even, it can be thought to exist in reality also, which is greater. If then that-than-which-a-greater-cannot-be-thought exists in the mind alone, this same that-than-which-a-greater-*cannot*-be thought is that-than-which-a-greater-*can*-be-thought. But this is obviously impossible. Therefore there is absolutely no doubt that something-than-which-a-greater-cannot-be-thought exists both in the mind and in reality.

10. Isaac Bashevis Singer, "Joy," in *Gimpel the Fool and Other Stories* (New York: Farrar, Straus & Giroux, 1957), pp. 131–132.

11. Elie Wiesel, *Four Hasidic Masters and Their Struggle against Melancholy* (Notre Dame, Ind.: University of Notre Dame Press, 1978), p. 14.

12. Ibid., p. 17.

13. Rabbi Barukh of Medzebozh, quoted in Wiesel, *Four Hasidic Masters*, p. 31.

14. Ibid., p. 43.

15. Ibid., p. 59.

16. Friedrich Nietzsche, *Thus Spoke Zarathustra*, trans. R. J. Hollingdale (Harmondsworth: Penguin, 1961), part IV (8), p. 331.

17. St. Hesychios the Priest, in *Philokalia* I, p. 186, no. 136.

18. Martin Buber, *Ten Rungs: Hasidic Sayings* (New York: Schocken, 1947), p. 42.

19. Robert J. Lifton, *The Broken Connection: On Death and the Continuity of Life* (New York: Simon and Schuster, 1980), p. 139.

20. Carol Ochs, *Women and Spirituality* (Totowa, N.J.: Rowman & Allanheld, 1983), p. 95.

21. Abraham Joshua Heschel, *Who Is Man?* (Stanford: Stanford University Press, 1965), p. 97.

22. Howard Thurman, *The Centering Moment* (Richmond: Friends United Press, 1969), p. 58.

23. Joseph H. Hertz, ed. and trans., *The Authorised Daily Prayer Book*, rev. ed. (New York: Bloch Publishing Co., 1957), p. 270.

24. Cf. Philip Birnbaum, ed. and trans., *Daily Prayer Book* (New York: Hebrew Publishing Co., 1949), pp. 134–136.

25. Abraham Joshua Heschel, *Man Is Not Alone: A Philosophy of Religion* (New York: Farrar, Straus & Giroux, 1951), p. 88.

26. Cf. Dante, *Inferno*, trans. John D. Sinclair (New York: Oxford University Press, 1939), canto I, p. 23.

27. Heschel, *Man Is Not Alone*, pp. 295–296.

2. EXPERIENCE

1. Heschel, *Quest for God*, p. 34.

2. Tu Wei-ming, *Neo-Confucian Thought in Action: Wang Yang-ming's Youth (1472–1509)* (Berkeley: University of California Press, 1976), p. ix.

3. Ibid., p. 59.

4. Thomas Merton, *The Way of Chuang Tzu* (New York: New Directions, 1969), p. 11.

5. Joanna Field, *A Life of One's Own* (Los Angeles: J. P. Tarcher, 1981).

6. Howard Thurman, *With Head and Heart: The Autobiography of Howard Thurman* (New York: Harcourt Brace Jovanovich, 1979), p. 270.

7. Marion Milner, *On Not Being Able to Paint* (New York: International Universities Press, 1957), p. 27.

8. Dorothy L. Sayers, in Dante, *The Divine Comedy*, trans. D. L. Sayers (Harmondsworth: Penguin, 1949), vol. 1, p. 95.

9. John Meagher, *The Gathering of the Ungifted: Toward a Dialogue on Christian Identity* (New York: Paulist Press, 1972), p. 110.

10. Howard Thurman, *Mysticism and the Experience of Love* (Wallingford, Pa.: Pendle Hill, 1961), pp. 17–18.

11. See Ana-Maria Rizzuto, *The Birth of the Living God: A Psychoanalytic Study* (Chicago: University of Chicago Press, 1979).

3. Symbols of Death and Life

1. Walter Kaufmann, *Life at the Limits* (New York: Reader's Digest Press, 1978), p. 123.

2. Lifton, *The Broken Connection*, p. 6.

3. John S. Dunne, *The Church of the Poor Devil: Reflections on a Riverboat Voyage and a Spiritual Journey* (New York: Macmillan, 1982; rpt. Notre Dame, Ind.: University of Notre Dame Press, 1983), p. 124.

4. Lewis Thomas, *The Medusa and the Snail: More Notes of a Biology Watcher* (New York: Bantam, 1979), pp. 11–12.

5. *The Book of Common Prayer* (New York: Church Pension Fund, 1945), p. 332.

4. Space

1. Stanley Keleman, *Living Your Dying* (New York: Random House, 1974), p. 26.

2. Heschel, *Man Is Not Alone*, pp. 266–267.

3. Johann Wolfgang von Goethe, "Der Schenke," in *West-östlicher Divan*, quoted in Martin Buber, *I and Thou*, 2d ed., trans. R. G. Smith (New York: Scribner's, 1958), p. xv.

4. Obadiah ben Jacob Sforno, quoted in W. Gunther Plaut, ed., *The Torah: A Modern Commentary* (New York: Union of American Hebrew Congregations, 1981), p. 86.

5. Carol Ochs, "Leah" (unpublished novel).

6. Samuel Terrien, *The Elusive Presence* (New York: Harper and Row, 1978), p. 1.

7. Ibid., p. 8.

5. TIME

1. Aristotle, *Physics* IV:11, 219a13–20, in *The Basic Works*, ed. Richard McKeon (New York: Random House, 1941), p. 291.
2. Rainer Maria Rilke, *Duino Elegies*, No. 9, quoted in Walter Kaufmann, *Time is an Artist* (New York: Reader's Digest Press, 1978), p. 36.
3. Mishnah, *Sanhedrin* 4:5, quoted in Plaut, *The Torah*, p. 24.
4. Terrien, *The Elusive Presence*, p. 77.
5. Heschel, *Man Is Not Alone*, p. 88.
6. Ibid., p. 284.

6. LOVE

1. Spinoza, *Ethics*, Part III: Definitions of the Emotions, VI and II.
2. Peter Hartocollis, *Time and Timelessness: The Varieties of Temporal Experience* (New York: International Universities Press, 1983), p. 59.
3. Ibid., p. 76.
4. Field, *A Life of One's Own*, chapter 7.
5. Spinoza, *On the Improvement of the Understanding*, p. 8.
6. Ibid., p. 3.
7. Cf. Martin Buber, *I and Thou*, 2d ed., trans. R. G. Smith (New York: Scribner, 1958).
8. John S. Dunne, *The Way of All the Earth: Experiments in Truth and Religion* (New York: Macmillan, 1972; rpt. Notre Dame, Ind.: University of Notre Dame Press, 1978), p. ix.
9. Dunne, *Church of the Poor Devil*, p. 61.
10. Ibid., p. 65.
11. Tu Wei-ming, *Neo-Confucian Thought in Action*, p. 143.
12. Martin Marty, *Friendship* (Allen, Tex.: Argus Communications, 1980), p. 24.
13. Ibid., p. 45.

14. Confucius, *The Analects*, trans. D. C. Lau (Harmondsworth: Penguin, 1979), 19:14 (p. 155).

15. Quoted in Abraham Joshua Heschel, *I Asked For Wonder: A Spiritual Anthology*, ed. Samuel H. Dresner (New York: Crossroad, 1983), p. viii.

16. Confucius, *Analects* 7:30 (p. 90).

17. Abraham Joshua Heschel, *The Insecurity of Freedom: Essays In Human Existence* (New York: Farrar, Straus & Giroux, 1967), p. 102.

7. Life in Death

1. Robert S. Bilheimer, *A Spirituality for the Long Haul: Biblical Risk and Moral Stand* (Philadelphia: Fortress Press, 1984), p. 19.

2. Ibid., p. 84.

3. Jean Paul Sartre, *Existentialism*, trans. B. Frechtman (New York: Philosophical Library, 1947), p. 22–23.

4. Terrien, *The Elusive Presence*, p. xxvii.

5. Heschel, *Man Is Not Alone*, p. 88.

6. Basil Mitchell, "Theology and Falsification," in *Religion from Tolstoy to Camus*, ed. Walter Kaufmann (New York: Harper & Row, 1961), p. 476.

7. See, for example, Birnbaum, *Daily Prayer Book*, p. 72.

8. Quoted in Harry Emerson Fosdick, *The Meaning of Faith* (New York: Associated Press, 1922), p. 273.

9. Confucius, *Analects*, 7:20 (p. 88).

10. Heschel, *Man Is Not Alone*, p. 162.

11. Carol Ochs, "Prayer on a New Home" (unpublished).

8. Universe As Home

1. Milner, *On Not Being Able to Paint*, p. 27.

2. John S. Dunne, *Reasons of the Heart* (New York: Macmillan, 1978; rpt. Notre Dame, Ind.: University of Notre Dame Press, 1979), p. 94.

About the Author

C arol Ochs is Professor and Chairperson of the Department of Philosophy at Simmons College, Boston. She studied at the City College of New York and received her M.A. and Ph.D. from the City University of New York and Brandeis University, respectively. Her previous works are *Behind the Sex of God* and *Women and Spirituality*. She is married and has two daughters.